What You Were Never Meant to See

The Systems of Access, Compatibility, and Post-Democratic Control

James Ergle

Copyright © 2025 by James Ergle

All rights reserved.

No part of this publication may be reproduced, distributed, or transmitted in any form or by any means, including photocopying, recording, or other electronic or mechanical methods, without the prior written permission of the author, except in the case of brief quotations used in critical reviews, commentary, or educational use.

This book is independently published by the author.

Printed and distributed via IngramSpark (paperback and hardcover).

Ebook edition and print available through Amazon Kindle.

Cover design and interior layout by the author.

For more work by the author, visit:

https://radicalleanings.substack.com

First edition: 2025

ISBN: 9798998989636

Table of Contents

Introduction..3
You Don't Like Soda. You Like the Bite..5
Caffeine Isn't Waking You Up. It's Paying Off a Debt It Created..............10
Your Phone Isn't Addicting You. It's Training You to Beg for Signals.....15
You Thought That Wall Was Blank..21
Clean Design as Interface Control..27
You Don't Own Anything. You're Renting Your Own Life....................34
They Could Make It Last. They Just Don't......................................38
Why Your School Had a Bell..42
Behavioral Fencing: The Architecture of Micro-Control....................46
Compliance Scripts: How Systems Write You Before You Act..................49
Credit Scores as Behavioral Scaffolding...52
Consumer Debt as a Behavioral Leash..58
Gamification and Loyalty Loops..63
Religion and Wellness as Identity Scripts..68
Work-Life Balance as Corporate Myth..73
Manufactured Movements...78
Education as Behavioral Blueprint...83
Student Loans and the School-to-Debt Pipeline................................89
Healthcare as a Compliance Gatekeeper..94
The Mental Health Awareness PR Loop...100
Workplace Surveillance and Biometric Productivity Tools...............105
Compliance Scripts..110
The Vocabulary of Obedience...114
Poverty Rebranded as "Personal Responsibility"............................119
"Middle Class" as a Manufactured Identity....................................124
Social Media as Self-Surveillance Theater......................................128
Default Erosion of Privacy as the New Normal..............................133
Neutrality as a Weapon..138
The Leash You Voted For..143
The Bilderberg Template..148
The World Economic Forum and Preemptive Narrative Management.....153
Think Tanks and War..158
The NGO–Intel Feedback Loop...163
The Price of Rescue...168
The Control Grid..173
Big Tech as Policy Architects...176
The Surveillance Web..181

The Black Budget State..186
Continuity of Government (COG)..191
CBDCs as Financial Fencing...195
Opting out of Existence..199
Digital Identity as Enforcement Substrate...204
Algorithmic Visibility and Digital Erasure...208
Military-Corporate Media After 9/11..213
Cultural Exports as Global Alignment...218
Climate Narratives and Sustainability as Soft Governance......................222
Trade Law Harmonization as Regulatory Capture...................................227
The Operating Layer..234
Pushing Back: What This Book Gets Wrong—and Why It Still Matters..239
Sources..248
About the Author..250

Introduction

This Book Refuses to Be Neutral

This is most certainly NOT a balanced book. It does not strive for neutrality. It does not pretend to present "both sides." It is not objective. It is not fair in the traditional sense.

This book is biased. That is intentional.

It was written by someone who has spent years inside the systems that most people only see from the outside. I have watched them fail, not by accident, but by design. I am not documenting them as an impartial observer. I am dragging them into the light as someone who sees the pattern. My goal is not to gently describe these control structures. My goal is to strip them of their disguises. I am not neutral. I am angry.

If you are looking for a tidy policy review or a technocrat's white paper, you will not find it here. What you will find is a polemic. It was shaped to wake up readers who have been lulled into compliance by the familiar. The systems that surround us, normalize us, and script us do not announce themselves. They do not need to. They are elegant, frictionless, and polite. And that is exactly why they need to be challenged by a voice that refuses politeness.

This book leans hard into its narrative. Sometimes it leans too hard. There are moments where emotion overtakes precision, where a metaphor cuts deeper than a dataset would. I am aware of this. You should be too.

But if you read carefully, you will see that each chapter builds on evidence. The point is not to prove a grand conspiracy. The point is to reveal a pattern. It's one that emerges from shared incentives, reinforcing structures, and normalized defaults. These patterns limit your autonomy while pretending to empower it.

In my last book, I avoided logical fallacies with almost religious discipline. I wanted every argument to hold up in court. This time, the courtroom is the culture itself. That calls for a different strategy. It requires a louder voice. It requires accepting some imperfection in service of urgency.

This does not mean I am immune to criticism. In fact, I collected every fallacy, every overreach, and every speculative leap this book makes. I addressed them directly in a chapter at the end. Not to weaken the argument, but to sharpen it. If you want to see where this book falters and why it still matters, I suggest you read that chapter too.

Because the point of this book is not to win a debate. The point is to break a trance.

And sometimes, that means raising your voice.

You Don't Like Soda. You Like the Bite.

How carbonation hacks your brain while no one notices—or cares.

You think you like soda because it tastes good. You don't. You like it because it bites you, and your brain likes being bitten. Just a little. This isn't about sugar and we'll get to caffeine in the next chapter. Right now, we're talking about carbonation, the part you never think about.

That crisp burn at the back of the throat, the rush behind your nose, and the sharp snap of the can opening are all sensations. But none of them are flavor. It is pain. Mild, contained, chemically induced pain. The kind that dances right up to the edge of discomfort, then folds back into pleasure before your brain can complain. You think it is refreshment. It is not. It is reinforcement. And you are not the first person to fall for it.

I. When Bubbles Were Medicine

In 1767, a clergyman and chemist named Joseph Priestley discovered carbonation by accident. He hung a bowl of water over a beer vat and watched it fizz. He called the result "impregnated water" and believed it could prevent scurvy. To him, it was a medical tonic. A curiosity. A tool. He shared it with friends and wrote about how "peculiarly refreshing" it felt. But he never once thought it might be habit-forming. The science of addiction did not exist. There were no dopamine models, no behavioral loops, no language to describe the hook that carbonation would become. Priestley wasn't trying to sell a feeling. He was trying to bottle a cure.

II. Schweppe Sells the Sensation

By 1783, a man named Jacob Schweppe figured out how to manufacture carbonated water at scale. He founded the Schweppes company and turned Priestley's experiment into a product. What did Schweppe do differently? He made it shelf-stable, bottled it beautifully, and branded it as healthful and refined. He wasn't selling chemistry. He was selling status.

And while he could not describe carbonation in neurological terms, he did not need to. He had behavior. Customers paid more for fizzy than for flat. They called it invigorating. They kept coming back. He optimized for what worked. That was exploitation, even without explanation.

III. Syrup and Seduction

In the 1800s, pharmacists began adding syrups to carbonated water in the form of cola, root beer, and sarsaparilla. Soda fountains were often inside drugstores. The syrups weren't just sweet. They were laced with cocaine, morphine, caffeine, quinine, and sugar.

That's when soda became something more than refreshment. It became a habit. Carbonation wasn't the drug. It was the delivery system. It sharpened the sweetness, boosted the caffeine, and built a link between physical sensation and psychological reward. Soda became social, comforting, slightly transgressive. A daily jolt that felt earned.

They did not have the science to explain it. But they did not need it. They had lines out the door.

IV. The Loop Is Now Engineered

Today, soda companies absolutely know what they are doing. They have filed patents on effervescence control to optimize the impact of the first sip. They study mouthfeel and neural response. Coca-Cola refers to the crack–fizz–sip experience as a brand ritual in internal agency briefs.

This isn't speculation. It is product design.

The carbonation activates your TRPA1 receptors, the same ones stimulated by mustard or wasabi. What it delivers is not flavor, and it is not nutrition. It delivers stimulation. This sensation is paired with sugar, caffeine, and acid to create a tightly constructed behavioral loop: cue, craving, response, reward.

But make no mistake. This is not a sugar essay, and it is not a caffeine essay. Those are different creatures. This one is about the fizz, the bite, and the trigger built entirely from bubbles.

It is a micropleasure: a small, carefully engineered burst of sensation. It is fast, fleeting, and just satisfying enough to make you reach for the next one.

V. Hidden in Plain Sight

There is no scandal here. No secret lab. Just ordinary manipulation hidden in everyday language: crisp, refreshing, tingly, a little bite, it just hits different.

These are euphemisms for sensory control. Defanged phrases that keep you from asking questions. It's not that you weren't told. It's that the language made you stop caring.

That is how most modern manipulation works. It is not buried. It is normalized. Hidden not by secrecy, but by routine. By branding. By nostalgia.

This is not an accident but a choice in form.

VI. Is There Any Legitimate Benefit?

This would all be more forgivable if carbonation offered something useful. But what does it actually do for you?

It does not hydrate you better. It does not nourish you. It does not improve digestion in any meaningful way. Some claim it helps with satiety or bloating. Maybe. But peppermint tea and sitting upright work better. They also don't come engineered for craving.

Even the supposed "fullness" from fizzy water is just gas expansion. It fades fast. And yes, this includes sparkling water and seltzer. The sugar is optional. The bite is the product.

So why are we drinking it?

Because we have been trained to. Because it feels normal. Because everything else feels flat. There is no nutritional logic. No survival function. No meaningful health payoff.

We drink carbonation because it feels like something is happening. Because it fills fleeting moments with engineered sensation. Because we have been taught that stimulation means satisfaction.

It is not hydration. It is theater.

VII. So What?

If carbonation can train your brain to crave pain, what else has been normalized under the label of pleasure? What other loops have you accepted as refreshing, comforting, or earned, without ever questioning who benefits from your craving?

You do not have to quit soda. But you should notice the bite. Not because it is dangerous. Because it is training you. And the next loop might not be fizzy. It might be bright. Or sweet. Or shaped like a notification.

Caffeine Isn't Waking You Up. It's Paying Off a Debt It Created.

How the most accepted drug on Earth built the quietest dependency in history.

You think caffeine gives you energy. It doesn't. It just makes withdrawal feel like relief. That jolt you feel after coffee is not clarity. It is the fog lifting from a deficit caffeine created in the first place. You are not becoming alert. You are returning to baseline. And it will not last. Because caffeine doesn't give. It borrows.

I. The Great Trick

Caffeine blocks adenosine receptors in your brain. Adenosine is the chemical that tells your body it is time to rest. When caffeine blocks it, your brain keeps firing, and you feel alert. But the adenosine does not go away. It builds up in the background. The longer it is blocked, the harder it crashes when the caffeine wears off.

So you drink more. And you do not feel better. You just feel normal until it wears off again. Caffeine does not energize you. It rents your alertness back to you at interest. Or think of it as a treadmill. It feels like motion. But it doesn't move you forward.

II. This Isn't About a Cup of Tea

This is not about a mild dose of green tea. This is about concentrated caffeine found in coffee, soda, energy drinks, and pills, all delivered in forms designed for consistency and speed. These are not just beverages. They are compliance systems. They are marketed as performance tools and embedded into morning rituals so thoroughly that skipping them can feel like failure. The purpose is not enjoyment. The purpose is reliability.

III. How It Became Normal

Caffeine did not rise on its own. Its spread was directly tied to productivity. In the early 20th century, factory owners provided coffee to workers to reduce fatigue and minimize break times. It made people more alert, more compliant, and easier to manage. When white-collar work replaced industrial labor, caffeine came with it. It was no longer treated as a luxury; it became an expectation.

The idea that people should feel tired mid-morning was reframed as a personal failing. Coffee became a self-management tool. Over time, it lost its association with ritual and became part of the timeclock. No one questioned it, because everyone was tired.

IV. The Modern Formula

First came soda. Then energy drinks. After that, caffeine pills and focus shots entered the market. They were followed by nootropic gummies, stimulant-infused toothpaste, and so-called "clean energy" drinks containing up to 300 milligrams of caffeine per can. The dosage increased. The delivery sped up. The branding became more refined. And gradually, the product itself transformed.

The real product is not caffeine. It is the permission to keep functioning. You are not drinking to wake up. You are drinking to delay collapse. That collapse may be emotional, hormonal, or physical. The caffeine does not resolve it. It simply postpones it.

V. What Caffeine Actually Does

Caffeine blocks your ability to feel fatigue. It increases cortisol and adrenaline. It temporarily sharpens focus but depletes recovery. It alters sleep architecture for six to twelve hours, even when consumed early in the day. It reduces sleep quality, delays melatonin release, and increases nighttime wakefulness.

A 2013 study in the *Journal of Clinical Sleep Medicine* found that caffeine taken six hours before bed reduced total sleep time by more than an hour and delayed melatonin production by about forty minutes. These effects are not dramatic. That is what makes them dangerous. You will not crash your car. You will not hallucinate. You will just keep going, even when you should stop.

That is what makes it perfect.

VI. Why Quitting Feels Like Failing

If you quit caffeine for two to five days, you will likely experience headaches, irritability, fatigue, brain fog, and a low mood. That feels like a sign that something is wrong with you. But it isn't. It is a correction. You are not broken. You are rebalancing. The withdrawal is not a flaw. It is the loop exposing itself.

Caffeine does not improve your energy. It shifts the cost. It delays fatigue, then sells you relief from the delay. That is why people crash. That is why people relapse. The drug is not just in the bloodstream. It is in the baseline.

VII. The System Needs You Awake

Caffeine is not an indulgence. It functions as a layer of control. It is ubiquitous not because it serves your needs, but because it serves the needs of the system. When you are tired at work, you take a pill. When you are tired at school, you reach for a can. When exhaustion sets in during parenting, you increase your dose. This pattern is not a sign of personal failure. It is the result of deliberate design.

We are not encouraged to pause. We are conditioned to override. The system is not built to accommodate your limits. It is built to stretch them.

Caffeine does not exist in isolation. It is part of a larger system, much like nicotine and sugar, that rewards people for staying alert and remaining compliant. Its influence is not only chemical. It is also deeply cultural.

VIII. The Micropleasure of Control

Caffeine is not only a stimulant. It is a ritual. The sound of the machine. The smell of the roast. The warmth of the mug. The feel of the can. The label that promises "zero crash." These are not incidental features. They are part of the loop.

Caffeine is a micropleasure. It provides a brief illusion of control. It creates the sensation of being alert, competent, and composed, even when none of those things are actually true. Caffeine does not make you functional. It makes you feel functional. That feeling is the real product being sold.

IX. So What?

If caffeine can mask fatigue and sell the mask as energy, what else are we calling performance? What other substances and habits have been repackaged as empowerment when they are really just tools for extending output?

You do not have to quit caffeine. But stop pretending it is power.

Try this: skip it for three days. Watch what happens. Watch how much of your routine falls apart. Watch who profits from your recovery.

That is where your energy is going.

Your Phone Isn't Addicting You. It's Training You to Beg for Signals.

How notification systems hijack ancient survival instincts and call it connection.

I. What You Think You Know

Most people believe they already understand social media manipulation. They've heard the word "dopamine" enough times to assume the problem is chemical and self-contained. Apps are "addictive," they say, and the solution is less screen time. But that framing leaves out the most important part. Dopamine is not the enemy. It is the delivery system. The manipulation goes deeper into the very evolutionary survival code that still governs how human beings interpret silence, attention, and exclusion.

Notifications do more than trigger pleasure. They mimic social signals. Your brain does not crave the alert because it is entertaining. It craves the alert because it is seeking reassurance that you have not been abandoned. The moment a badge appears or a ping sounds on your phone, your body relaxes, even slightly. You have been acknowledged. You are still part of the group. But when nothing arrives, and the feed stays quiet for too long, what you feel is not boredom. What you feel is a sense of threat. You feel danger.

II. The Tribe Was the Lifeline

Humans did not evolve to be alone. We survived in groups, usually no more than 150 people. Anthropologist Robin Dunbar found that our brains are wired to track and maintain about that many social relationships. Inside these groups, signaling was essential. A glance, a sound, or a name spoken aloud were never just gestures. They were signals of inclusion. If no one spoke to you, there was no help coming. If no one saw you, you did not eat. The brain learned to track signs of connection and to treat silence as a potential threat.

Social media platforms did not invent this system. They hijacked it. They took brief, evolution-shaped communication signals that once indicated safety and digitized them. These signals were then embedded into a reinforcement loop. The result is not a platform designed to inform. It is a system built to condition. It teaches users to feel seen at unpredictable moments and to experience silence as something unbearable that must be escaped.

III. The Intermittent Reward Schedule

In the 1950s, behavioral psychologist B.F. Skinner discovered that the most powerful way to shape behavior was not by offering consistent rewards, but by using variable ones. When a reward appears every time, it quickly loses its effect. But when the reward is unpredictable and arrives only occasionally, the subject becomes fixated. This principle has been applied to slot machines, gambling apps, and more recently, social media notifications.

Modern research supports this. A 2020 study in *Computers in Human Behavior* found that unpredictable notification timing increased anxiety, checking behavior, and perceived importance of alerts. Platforms deliberately delay, withhold, or batch alerts. Not to make them more useful, but to make them more compelling. Your brain is not checking for updates. It is waiting for relief. The loop is not driven by content, but by uncertainty. You never know what kind of signal is coming next, or when.

That uncertainty makes the signal more important than its meaning.

Most major platforms now use backend algorithms to decide *when* you receive a notification, not just what it says. You might get three likes instantly, but the app holds two back to push later, spacing them out to keep your brain checking. Some platforms even delay notifications if you've been inactive too long to deliberately create a spark of perceived urgency to pull you back in. The goal isn't to inform you. It's to interrupt you just enough to re-engage the loop.

IV. Silence as Threat

A phone that stays silent is not a neutral object. It becomes a source of tension. Over time, the absence of notifications begins to feel like being overlooked or even rejected. This is not metaphorical. Research by Naomi Eisenberger and Matthew Lieberman showed that social exclusion activates the same region of the brain as physical pain. When too much time passes without interaction, whether real or simulated, the body interprets that silence as a sign of vulnerability.

Most users do not consciously fear being ignored, but the stress response shows up anyway. There is a reason you feel compelled to open your phone even when you know there is nothing new. There is a reason you reread messages, refresh feeds, and loop back through apps. You are not seeking entertainment. You are seeking confirmation that you still exist within a network. The notification is not a message. It is a signal of safety.

V. Obligation as Interface

Social media does not just exploit your need for inclusion. It exploits your instinct for reciprocity. In healthy human communities, signals were mutual. A gesture received required a gesture returned. You helped who helped you. You responded to those who acknowledged you. This was not politeness. It was survival.

Platforms exploit that instinct to drive engagement. Every like becomes a prompt to respond, and every comment feels like a signal you are expected to acknowledge. This expectation is not rooted in social etiquette, but in the internal logic of the platform. You do not want to leave others waiting. You do not want to appear cold or unresponsive. As the number of signals increases, so does the pressure to maintain them. What may have started as simple sharing quickly shifts into performance. Your identity becomes something you must manage, and each notification turns into a loose thread that demands your attention before it begins to unravel.

That pressure compounds fast. You like someone's post, they like yours. You comment, they expect a reply. Before long, you're not responding out of interest, but out of maintenance. You're managing impressions, not relationships, and the platform reinforces this by highlighting unanswered comments, boosting recent interactions, and tracking your response time like a metric.

VI. Signals Are Expensive

In the animal world, signaling is costly. Birds sing, peacocks display, primates groom. These actions take time and energy, and they carry risk. But they also build social rank and cohesion. Humans have the same instinct, and social media turns it into currency.

A status update is not a neutral event. It is a public signal. Every post you make, whether you realize it or not, is shaped to communicate who you are, what you value, and how you want others to respond. This creates a cycle in which attention becomes addictive, not because it brings pleasure, but because it begins to feel essential. If you stop signaling, you risk becoming invisible. So you post again. You edit. You rehearse. You become your own content manager, sustaining a system that never runs out of space and never stops watching.

And now the tribe is not 150 people. It is everyone. You are signaling to strangers, to algorithms, to invisible audiences whose expectations change by the hour. One day you are rewarded for honesty. The next day you are punished for it. The rules shift, but the pressure to perform remains constant. Uncertainty intensifies the loop.

VII. Designed to Disrupt

This did not happen by accident. It was built. The people who created social media studied behavioral conditioning, evolutionary psychology, and slot-machine logic. They knew how to manipulate attention, and they used that knowledge to keep users active, uncertain, and emotionally exposed.

Notifications are not real-time communication tools. They are behavioral triggers. They interrupt work, sleep, meals, and conversations, not because they are urgent, but because they are effective. They keep you looking. They keep you reacting. They break your focus, then offer themselves as the solution to the distraction they caused.

The system does not care what you do, as long as you do it inside the loop.

VIII. So What?

This is not just about screen time. It is about a system that has taken the most ancient parts of your brain, the parts responsible for safety, belonging, and communication, and turned them into a product. This system is not hidden. It is visible. You participate in it every time you reach for the phone in your pocket without knowing why.

You do not have to quit social media. You do not have to turn off your phone. But try this: turn off your notifications for 24 hours. Not just one app, but all of them. Then watch what happens. Notice how often your hand still reaches. Notice the flicker of tension. That is not a habit. That is training.

And someone is making money every time you respond to it.

You Thought That Wall Was Blank

Ambient Advertising and the Disappearance of Consent

I. The Ads You Didn't See

Not every ad is meant to be noticed.

Ambient advertising doesn't compete for your attention. It bypasses it. It's not a pop-up or a jingle. It's a branded scent in a store's ventilation system, a glowing trash can in an airport, or a screen talking to you at the gas pump. You're not supposed to remember the ad. You're supposed to absorb the environment it shapes.

Traditional advertising asks for your attention. Ambient advertising installs itself in your environment. It turns neutral space into a delivery mechanism. And because it doesn't announce itself, most people don't push back. They just adapt.

II. Consent Isn't What It Used to Be

There's a difference between walking into a branded space and being surrounded by advertising you can't avoid. A Subway restaurant is commercial by nature, but you didn't choose to receive twelve brand impressions with your sandwich. Your napkin, your cup, your lid, your wrapper, your bag, your tray liner, your receipt, your loyalty app, and every surface in the store carry a logo. The repetition isn't accidental. It's strategic.

The issue isn't visibility. It's erosion of consent. At a gas pump, you didn't ask for the screen to play ads while you're trapped by the nozzle. You didn't opt in to elevator screens or scent-masked clothing stores. These are captive zones: locations where attention is constrained and choice is limited. Ambient advertising flourishes here because you can't easily escape it.

III. The Branded Environment

Ambient advertising operates through presence, not persuasion.

Abercrombie & Fitch's retail strategy in the 2000s included pumping its "Fierce" cologne into store HVAC systems, triggering scent-based memory associations in teenage shoppers. A 2005 article in *AdAge* explained that the tactic increased dwell time and repeat visits. Coca-Cola deployed motion-sensitive vending machines that flash lights or greetings as pedestrians pass that were designed to subtly boost brand recall through reactive stimuli. A 2018 Journal of Consumer Research study found such interactive cues raised brand recognition by 12% over static machines.

Disney sponsored live weather segments on local news broadcasts in 2015 and not just the commercial breaks, but the actual weather. Your forecast came framed in castle motifs.

This is not traditional advertising. It is what David Ogilvy referred to as "total environmental branding," a method of embedding the brand into physical space until it becomes indistinguishable from the environment itself.

IV. When the Ad Doesn't Look Like an Ad

Ambient ads don't look like persuasion. They look like setting.

A QR code printed as graffiti. A Nike message painted on subway steps. A motivational phrase etched into the running path by a shoe brand. These aren't interruptions. They're decor. That's not accidental. The less it looks like marketing, the deeper it sinks. And that's why they work.

When advertising is decorative, it stops registering as external influence. It becomes texture. It's just another part of the architecture. You don't resist the message because you no longer recognize it as one.

The ad isn't a pitch anymore. It's background.

V. Advertising as Infrastructure

The goal isn't for you to buy something. The goal is for the ad to become normal.

The vending machine doesn't need to be persuasive. It just needs to be everywhere. A trash can with a logo doesn't need to convert you. It just needs to occupy the same space every day until your brain stops seeing it.

This is the point where ambient advertising transforms into infrastructure. Walls, floors, tables, trash cans, basically every surface becomes monetizable. Major advertising firms such as Ogilvy, Grey, and Leo Burnett are not simply placing campaigns anymore. They are purchasing physical space and selling long-term brand presence. Retailers like Subway and tech companies like Uber collaborate with these agencies to saturate public environments with repeated, low-resistance brand impressions. These efforts are not evaluated by how many people make immediate purchases. Instead, they are measured by how well the message is retained and how easily it can be recalled.

The motive isn't mystery. It's revenue.

This shift isn't happening in isolation. City governments and transit authorities often enter partnerships with branding firms in exchange for funding, free infrastructure upgrades, or maintenance contracts. Advertising isn't just tolerated, it's traded. A logo on a bench might pay for a streetlight. A branded charging station might offset budget shortfalls. The result is a public environment shaped by private interests, where the line between city planning and brand presence begins to dissolve.

VI. Public Space, Private Control

Some spaces are optional. Others aren't.

A mall can be avoided. A gas station, not so easily. Transit systems, elevators, airport gates, restrooms, and other confined public spaces function as captive zones, where your ability to exit is limited and your attention is naturally constrained. Ambient advertising thrives in these environments because it does not require active engagement. That is why it appears in these places first.

In 2020, a campaign by JCDecaux placed branded touchpoints throughout 18 major European train stations. These included benches, stairwells, and even charging ports. The stated goal was "environmental imprinting," a term the company used in its own pitch materials.

This isn't about aesthetics. It's about zoning. The branding reaches you because you have nowhere else to go.

VII. Some People Resist

Not everyone accepts this passively.

On TikTok, hashtags like #AdFail and #BrandOverload mock logo-saturated packaging and try-hard corporate slogans. Some people peel off branding stickers, draw mustaches on ad posters, or record elevator screen rants. Defacing ads is still an act of resistance, even when it's small.

But for most people, resistance wears down. The more often you see a branded napkin or glowing ad screen, the more normal it feels. Eventually, it stops provoking. It just becomes part of the room.

That's the success metric: invisibility through familiarity.

VIII. Symbols That Swallowed Reality

Baudrillard described a world in which signs no longer point to meaning. They become meaning. Ambient advertising lives there. This is why a Starbucks logo doesn't just mean coffee. It means warmth, familiarity, even safety for some people. The product becomes secondary. The logo is the experience. That's not by accident. It's the brand's entire survival strategy.

It does not reference a product. It is the product. A scent is not trying to sell you cologne. It is training your body to feel nostalgic the next time you encounter it. A projection on a sidewalk is not just promoting a brand. It is teaching you that even the ground you walk on can be sold.

The advertising doesn't interrupt. It frames. That's the difference.

IX. Branding Has Become the Default Texture

Your spaces aren't just surrounded by ads. They carry branding by default.

It's on your cup, your receipt, your pump, your screen, your route. It's stitched into your movements, not with slogans but with ambient repetition. There's no need for a call to action. Just saturation. Just permanence.

This isn't subversion. It's optimization that's been designed to monetize stillness.

X. Say It Out Loud

Ambient ads work because you don't notice them. But you can start by noticing one.

The next time you see a screen at the gas pump, a branded trash can, a QR code painted on the sidewalk try naming it. Say out loud: that's an ad. That's not infrastructure. That's influence. Naming it breaks the spell.

Then go further. Peel one off. Cover one up. Deface one. Break the brand's grip for just a second. The blank wall starts there.

Clean Design as Interface Control

Why frictionless systems aren't neutral—they're filters

I. The Disappearance of the Interface

Modern interfaces are designed to vanish.

They call it user-centered, minimalist, frictionless. But the result is that you see less, choose less, and understand less. Buttons become icons. Settings become layers. Functions disappear behind gestures or friendly prompts. You're not supposed to explore anymore. You're supposed to comply.

Apple's Human Interface Guidelines encourage designers to prioritize "clarity," "deference," and "depth." These sound empowering. But in practice, they justify flattening the interface until nothing is legible. "Deference" means silence. "Depth" means burying power. The user is meant to move smoothly through the system but not to inspect it.

Earlier interfaces were ugly, but honest. Drop-down menus showed every option. Installers let you pick what got installed. You could break things, but you could also understand them. Today's interfaces aren't just polished, they're also sealed.

II. Minimalism Is Just Propaganda for Big Small

Minimalism didn't start as a tool of control. It became one because it works.

In design circles, minimalism is framed as benevolence. It promises reducing friction, simplifying access, decluttering the mind. And it can do those things. But minimalism also removes power. It lets companies conceal options while looking helpful. It hides behavioral funnels behind elegance.

Minimalism is just propaganda for Big Small. It makes billion-dollar platforms look humble. It makes limited systems feel curated. It makes control look clean. The simpler the surface, the less you notice what's missing.

This isn't always malicious. Some designers genuinely want to help users. But in large systems, especially those driven by shareholder incentives, minimalism takes on an instrumental role.

It reduces cognitive resistance. It makes behavior predictable. It serves business models that depend on metrics like retention, engagement, and click-through.

Apple, Google, Meta, Amazon all rely on guiding users through high-conversion pathways. Minimalist interfaces do that. They remove distraction, yes. But they also remove exit routes.

III. The Hidden Option That Wasn't Supposed to Be Clicked

The most common form of control today is presence without visibility.

The options still exist. But you aren't meant to see them. Custom install paths are hidden behind tiny links. Opt-out settings are buried under four nested menus. Your location toggle is visible but are your background app permissions? Those are two swipes and three taps away.

This is standard practice, often called progressive disclosure, the design principle of showing only the "relevant" features at any given time. But who defines relevance? Not the user.

According to UX research by the Nielsen Norman Group, hiding advanced options leads most users to never discover them at all. That's not a side effect. It's a feature. If 90% of people won't touch what they can't see, you can technically claim transparency while achieving invisibility.

And over time, users stop looking. They assume that what's presented is what exists. The rest fades from awareness.

IV. Interfaces That Simulate Freedom

Postmodern theory predicted a world where symbols replace reality. We're living it.

Your interaction with software is now interaction with a simulation. The interface doesn't just represent the system. It replaces it. What you see is what you think exists. The choices are pre-filtered, the routes pre-designed, the output constrained. But it feels like freedom because the design is clean.

Canva feels empowering because it reduces design to a series of drag-and-drop choices, but every option you encounter has already been chosen by someone else. Photoshop, by contrast, opens with a blank canvas and no suggestions. The difference isn't aesthetic or emotional. It's structural. One platform offers freedom shaped by possibility; the other offers creativity constrained by predefined paths. Canva curates. Photoshop permits.

Modern software favors simulations of control. The user is given just enough flexibility to feel empowered but not enough to meaningfully alter the system.

V. The Corridor Model

The dominant UI pattern in consumer tech is not a dashboard. It's a corridor.

You're guided through suggestions, nudged by defaults, and kept moving with auto-fill prompts. Each step feels frictionless because it is designed that way. The system nudges, filters, hides. It lets you feel like you're exploring, but there's only one lit path at a time.

E-commerce platforms show "what's popular" instead of what's available. Streaming apps autoplay the next item. AI tools default to safe, vague outputs with no controls unless you click "Advanced." Even then, your freedom is still sandboxed.

Apple's ecosystem is notorious for this. iOS doesn't want you adjusting file structures. It doesn't want you switching default apps. It wants you gliding through a curated experience. And it's not alone. Android, once the more open system, has slowly adopted the same design metaphors: swipes over settings, gestures over menus, recommendations over directories.

Yes, power-user tools still exist. Blender, GIMP, Obsidian, and Linux offer depth and freedom, but they are niche. The mainstream corridor has already been built. Most users never leave it.

VI. The Incentive, Not the Villain

There is no mastermind here. Just market logic.

The problem isn't one person or company. The problem is the incentive structure. Clean design reduces complaints. It funnels attention. It lowers friction and raises engagement. It performs well in A/B tests. It makes investors happy. And that's enough.

Interfaces aren't being built to disempower users because of ideology. They're being built to increase retention, reduce cost, and support platforms that don't want you to leave. If removing 40% of user options improves engagement by 3%, that's the winning design.

That's not theory. That's platform logic.

VII. User Agency Exists—But It's Work

Some users dig deeper. They change settings. They jailbreak phones. They edit config files. They install Linux, write scripts, build custom dashboards. These people exist and they matter.

But they're rare.

Most users don't resist the corridor because they don't even know it's a corridor. The friction isn't just technical, it's cultural. People have been trained to think that if a feature isn't visible, it must not be available. That's how behavioral design works: it shifts what we consider possible.

And even those who *could* resist often choose not to. Because the defaults work. They're designed to. That's the genius of it and the trap.

VIII. Real-World Parallels That Hold

Some critics roll their eyes when you compare a glossy app to a modern airport or glass office building. But the metaphor holds.

In both software and physical space, the logic is the same: reduce resistance, guide motion, discourage loitering, and prevent exploration. Airports now use ambient lighting, touchscreen kiosks, and minimal signage not for the sake of elegance, but because these elements help control the movement of people through space. Corporate campuses use glass and white space to signal prestige and prevent wandering.

Design isn't just visual. It's behavioral. And in both digital and real-world environments, "clean" has become shorthand for "controlled."

IX. What's Missing Is Still There

That's the trick. You're not being lied to. You're being filtered.

Modern systems don't eliminate power. They hide it. The download link is there but it's gray, and small, and off to the side. The advanced settings still exist but they're phrased as warnings, hidden under toggles, or absent from mobile altogether.

You are not supposed to feel restricted. You are supposed to feel taken care of. And most users do.

That's why it works.

X. Click the Gray Link

This isn't a call to arms. Just a call to notice.

The system didn't remove your choices. It buried them under polish. You still have some agency. You still have some tools. You just have to work harder to find them.

Click the gray link. Open the hidden menu. Swipe when you're not told to swipe. Look for the settings icon that was meant to be ignored.

The design may be clean. But that doesn't mean it's honest.

You Don't Own Anything. You're Renting Your Own Life.

How subscriptions, DRM, and hidden limits replaced permanence with permission

I. The Disappearance of Ownership

Not long ago, if you wanted a movie, a program, or a razor, you bought it. You paid once and it was yours. That model is dead. Today, you pay again and again and not because the product improved, but because ownership itself has been phased out. The shift didn't happen with a single event. It crept in through convenience, bundling, and auto-renewal checkboxes. The model is always the same: low monthly fee, easy entry, hard exit. It sounds like access. But it's debt. You don't own your tools anymore. You rent their permission to use them.

II. The Software Trap

Adobe set the tone. In 2013, it ended perpetual licenses for Photoshop and moved to a subscription-only model: Creative Cloud. You couldn't buy the program anymore. You could only rent it. Competitors followed. Microsoft pushed Office into the cloud. Intuit locked tax software behind annual gates. Each update removed a feature from the purchase tier and placed it behind a recurring fee. The logic was simple: extract payment not for innovation, but for continued access. Once software became a service, cutting off service became leverage. Cancel your subscription, and your files become uneditable or trapped in proprietary clouds. Digital Rights Management (DRM) enforces this shift from ownership to permission by criminalizing autonomy. Circumventing DRM, whether to play a movie you bought on another device or to back up an eBook, is illegal under the DMCA in the United States. This flips the script: the buyer becomes the violator. Even when no theft occurs, the act of restoring control over your purchase is framed as sabotage. DRM doesn't protect creators. It protects platforms. It ensures that even when you think you own something, access is only granted on terms you cannot negotiate and cannot legally override.

III. Movies That Disappear from Your Shelf

Streaming reinforced the illusion. It felt like freedom: thousands of titles, one low price. But the catalog was rented, not stable. Movies vanish without warning. Licensing deals expire. Censorship edits creep in quietly. You never really had a collection. You had a temporary hallway pass to someone else's vault. Digital purchases offered no protection. Apple and Amazon have both removed previously bought films from users' libraries due to rights changes. In 2022, Amazon deleted purchased Kindle e-books from users' libraries when publishers pulled rights. You paid for a license to access something that may no longer exist. The disc you used to own is now a ghost in the cloud. You don't have a library. You have a tether.

Even the platforms themselves can vanish. When Microsoft shut down its eBook store in 2019, every purchased book was deleted from customer libraries with refunds issued, but no option to keep the content. When Google Play Music closed, libraries were forcibly migrated to YouTube Music, with some files lost in the transition. In a permission-based system, your "purchases" vanish if the gatekeeper exits the market. Ownership isn't just rented, it's revocable. When the platform dies, your shelf burns with it.

IV. Subscribed to Necessity

Then came the subscriptions to reality. Shaving kits, laundry pods, groceries, toilet paper. Everything basic turned premium, then got slotted into monthly boxes. Algorithms track your usage to predict reordering, nudging you to stay subscribed. Amazon's Subscribe & Save predicts your grocery needs, locking you into auto-deliveries. The goal wasn't convenience. It was habituation. Get the customer to hand over control of the decision itself. If you don't cancel it, you must want it. If you skip a box, we'll pause and reoffer it next month. It's not just stuff anymore. It's behavioral conditioning. A razor isn't just a razor. It's a quiet contract to keep paying, one charge at a time, until you forget to stop. Subscriptions didn't stop at necessities. They invaded the machines you thought you owned.

V. Even Cars Want Rent Now

BMW tried to charge $18 a month for heated seats in markets like South Korea. Ford locked remote start behind a subscription. Tesla disables features by software unless you pay again to unlock them. These aren't upgrades. They're paywalls on capabilities already inside the machine. You paid for the hardware. But the company holds the keys. This is software-as-service metastasized. You bought the car. But they rent you the features.

This rent-based logic now extends to repair. Many devices, from phones to tractors, are designed to prevent user maintenance. Apple uses proprietary screws and serialized parts. John Deere restricts farm equipment diagnostics to authorized dealers. In both cases, ownership is functionally revoked: you paid for the object, but not the right to fix it. The result is enforced dependence. Without access to schematics, firmware, or compatible parts, users become renters in all but name. They are liable for breakdowns but barred from solutions. "Right to repair" legislation exists only because repair was taken away.

VI. The Logic of Forever Payments

The subscription model isn't a business innovation. It's a containment strategy. You're not supposed to escape. Each system is designed to make the cost of quitting higher than the cost of staying. Loyalty perks. Account histories. Lost progress. Interruption fees. Want to fix them? Glue, proprietary screws, and costly policies deter you. Human psychology is part of the product design. Netflix's auto-resume keeps you watching; Adobe's cancellation fees keep you paying. They don't need to hide it. They just normalize it. You're not their customer. You're their annuity. And the best annuity is the one that forgets it's leaking.

VII. They Called It Access. It Was Always Control.

They told you it was about flexibility. About paying only for what you use. But that was never true. What you really lost was permanence. Autonomy. The ability to opt out without penalty. They say it's what people want. But people don't ask for expiration dates on tools, or deletion risks on files, or heating subscriptions in winter. They claim subscriptions save money, but perpetual payments dwarf one-time costs. They sell convenience, but you're buying surrender. What people want is reliability. What corporations want is control. And now, one monthly charge at a time, they tighten their grip.

They Could Make It Last. They Just Don't.

The economic logic behind engineered decay and psychological obsolescence

I. The Bulb That Lasted Too Long

In 1924, the world's largest lightbulb manufacturers formed a secret agreement in Geneva. Osram, Philips, General Electric, and a handful of others created the Phoebus cartel, an international consortium with one purpose: to limit the lifespan of the incandescent bulb. Lightbulbs had steadily improved for decades, with some lasting over 2,500 hours. That was a problem. Durable bulbs meant fewer purchases. So the cartel imposed a strict cap: 1,000 hours, no more. Any company producing longer-lasting bulbs faced fines. Labs were ordered to reverse-engineer failure. Engineers complied. The cartel lasted until the late 1930s, but by then, the 1,000-hour norm had stuck. While industrial and specialty bulbs retained longer lifespans, the 1,000-hour cap became the standard for consumer lighting. More importantly, the mindset spread. Consumers didn't know it had been artificially imposed. They just thought lightbulbs wore out. And that's how it began: the normalization of engineered decay.

II. The Year Your Car Got Old Overnight

Planned obsolescence isn't always mechanical. Sometimes it's psychological. In the 1920s, General Motors president Alfred Sloan faced a problem: people weren't buying new cars. The vehicles they owned still worked. So GM introduced the annual model-year design. Slight tweaks to body shape, trim, or accessories created the illusion of progress. New models looked better. Older ones suddenly looked old. The car you had last year now marked you as behind. It wasn't broken. It was obsolete by suggestion. Sloan called it "dynamic obsolescence." The public called it style. Either way, it worked. Ford, which had resisted frequent design changes, was forced to adapt. Once psychological obsolescence was proven profitable, physical degradation became optional. Today, this logic drives phones, furniture, and fast fashion. Brands like Zara release new styles each week not because consumers need them, but because last week's look is already considered outdated. We don't throw things out because they fail. We throw them out because we're embarrassed to still have them.

III. The Battery That Was Never Yours

In 2003, a viral video titled "iPod's Dirty Secret" exposed Apple's non-replaceable battery design. Early iPods were sealed shut, their lithium batteries hardwired and short-lived. After about 18 months, most units stopped holding a charge. Apple offered no replacement program. Their solution was simple: buy a new one. After public outrage and a class-action lawsuit, Apple offered battery replacements for a fee. But the precedent was set. Devices no longer needed to break. They just needed to die quietly, on schedule. Today, the same pattern applies to AirPods, iPhones, and MacBooks. Components are soldered, glued, or locked behind proprietary screws. Want to fix them? Glue, proprietary screws, and costly policies deter you. The machine is yours in name only. Its functionality is theirs to control.

Apple's sealed devices were just the start. Other industries took the lockout model and ran with it.

IV. The Ink That Disappeared on Schedule

Printer manufacturers took the concept even further. Companies like HP and Epson began embedding chips in ink cartridges that disabled them after a fixed number of pages or a preset expiration date even if ink remained. Refilled cartridges or third-party replacements were blocked by firmware updates or warnings. HP called it a "security feature." Critics called it what it was: forced obsolescence. Lawsuits followed. In some countries, consumer protection agencies stepped in. But the business model stayed. HP's budget printers often cost less than their ink. The DeskJet 2755e, for instance, sells for around $60. Interestingly, a full ink refill can run $50 to $70. You're not buying a printer. You're buying into a toll system.

And it didn't stop with ink. The same tactics scaled up with the devices we use most.

V. The Phone That Grew Slower While You Slept

Smartphones, the most visible tech in daily life, brought planned obsolescence into the software era. In 2017, Apple admitted to throttling the performance of older iPhones via software updates. Their justification: preventing crashes from degraded batteries. Apple claimed it was risk management. But the secrecy, the timing, and the outcome all suggest something else. These patterns consistently push users toward upgrades. Whether through slowing processors, bloating storage, or dropping app compatibility, older phones become less usable long before they fail. And yet the phone still looks fine. It hasn't failed. It's been obsoleted by design.

VI. The Logic That Doesn't Need a Memo

The drain anecdote is apocryphal: the story of a company that built an uncloggable basement drain so effective they went out of business. There are no verified records. But the lesson remains. If you build something too well, you won't sell another. Somewhere along the line, industries absorbed that logic and ran with it. Today, obsolescence is not just accepted. It's expected. Consumers joke about it. We mourn the durability of old appliances. We admire the 20-year-old Toyota or the ancient refrigerator that still works. But we keep buying the new thing anyway. Not because we want to. Because we have to.

Manufacturers claim forced upgrades are the price of innovation. They say we demand the new. But they design the old to fail. And when the new model comes with the same battery, the same proprietary screws, and the same built-in expiry, it isn't innovation. It's choreography. There's no secret. It's just profit masquerading as progress. No memo is needed. Just inertia. We like to think we're making choices. But what we're really choosing between are expiration dates.

Why Your School Had a Bell

Obedience Training for the Age of Managed Time

I. The Bell Was Never for You

Every child grows up hearing it: the metallic ring, the abrupt buzz, the unmistakable signal that dictates what comes next. Sit. Stand. Change rooms. Line up. Wait. The school bell offers no explanation; it simply overrides whatever you're doing and declares that it's time to stop. Not because the lesson is over, but because the schedule demands it. Its purpose was never to support learning. It was built to manage bodies. In many ways, the bell was the first behavioral fence.

II. Time Was the First Lesson

The industrial revolution created a new kind of workforce. This one that didn't follow seasons, intuition, or rhythm. It needed people who obeyed clocks. Who could endure boredom. Who would show up on time, take breaks on cue, and stop working exactly when told.

Bells weren't invented to oppress students. They were installed to coordinate the chaos of hundreds of kids changing rooms, staying on schedule, following structure. But the effect is deeper than logistics. When a bell tells you when to think, when to stop, and when to move, the mechanism becomes the message. You learn to submit to the clock before you learn to question the material.

III. This System Was Designed—Not Discovered

In the early 1800s, Prussia built a state-run education system with explicit goals: uniformity, discipline, nationalism, and obedience. Its schools emphasized punctuality, drill-style repetition, and deference to authority. When Horace Mann toured Prussia in 1843, he was so impressed that he pushed to replicate its structure in Massachusetts. In his 1844 *Seventh Annual Report*, he praised their "order, system, and punctuality," urging Americans to adopt their model.

This wasn't covert. It was bureaucratic engineering. The model wasn't shaped by what helped children learn. It was shaped by what made them easier to govern. Prussia needed obedient citizens. Industrial America needed reliable workers. And both found the same solution.

IV. The Factory Was Just the First Client

It's popular to mock the "factory model of education" as overused, but it's not wrong. It's just incomplete.

The bell-and-schedule structure wasn't built solely for factories. It was, and still is, perfect for any job where people have to follow instructions under surveillance. That includes clerical work, customer service, logistics, and compliance-heavy offices. School didn't train kids for one type of job. It trained them for life under management.

And it still does.

V. What the Structure Actually Teaches

Some students thrive under routine. Some subjects require repetition. But school doesn't reward curiosity. It rewards compliance.

You ask permission to speak. You raise your hand to use the

bathroom. You shift focus every 45 minutes whether you're ready or not. You memorize fragmented material, then forget it after the test. You're evaluated not on depth, but on pace and obedience.

The result isn't just underwhelming education. It's behavioral normalization: people who are used to being told when to think, when to speak, and when to stop.

VI. The Curriculum Beneath the Curriculum

The real lessons of school aren't printed in the textbook. They're embedded in the structure.

Show up on time. Sit where you're told. Don't ask too many questions. Defer to authority even when it contradicts itself. Don't finish early. Don't lag behind. Don't argue when the bell rings. Learn to perform tasks on someone else's clock. Learn to confuse following instructions with doing well.

That's the hidden curriculum. It doesn't teach you how to learn. It teaches you how to behave inside a system that doesn't care if you understand anything as long as you finish it on time.

VII. Why the Model Still Holds

The factory is mostly gone. The schedule remains. Why?

Because it still works for those who maintain it. A 2020 Brookings report found that American education policy continues to center on standardized testing, bell schedules, and externally enforced pacing. These practices align more closely with managerial control than with meaningful learning. State boards and contractors like Pearson continue to reinforce time-based compliance because it's scalable, cost-efficient, and easy to quantify.

School doesn't prepare students to lead. It prepares them to conform to time discipline. And that makes them compatible with shift-based jobs, productivity dashboards, and meetings that start at nine and mean nothing.

VIII. Resistance Exists—Just Not at Scale

Some parents homeschool to avoid this structure. Montessori and Waldorf schools intentionally skip bells and rigid schedules. Some teachers let kids keep reading past the buzzer. Some districts experiment with block schedules and open learning environments.

But they're exceptions. Most students still spend thirteen years learning to obey the schedule. And by the time they're done, it feels natural to work on command, wait for permission, and measure success in segments.

That's the point. Resistance exists. But replication wins.

IX. How to Push Back—For Real

You can't fix the system this week. But you can weaken its grip.

Ask your district why learning ends on a bell. Request one flexible, student-driven period a week. Support teachers who violate the schedule for curiosity. Let your child finish a thought instead of stopping for a hallway transition. Question why time obedience is treated as virtue.

You're not fighting school. You're fighting unquestioned scheduling as moral law.

And every time you let a student ignore the bell, you win a little.

Behavioral Fencing: The Architecture of Micro-Control

How invisible defaults and smooth design create the most effective prison.

I. The System Was Never Silent

Most people imagine control as something overt: police, laws, bans. But the most effective systems don't demand obedience. They shape behavior long before disobedience becomes an option. This is the architecture of micro-control. Not one lever, but many. Not a central command, but an ambient system. One designed not to restrain forcefully, but to nudge endlessly. It doesn't shape what you do. It shapes what you want.

II. Reinforcement in Small Doses

Everywhere you turn, the system reinforces itself with small signals. Carbonation isn't just mouthfeel. It's a micropleasure loop. Caffeine doesn't give energy. It restores what the last dose stole. Notifications don't inform. They train you to chase feedback. These may not always be conspiracies, but they're refined for effect. Coca-Cola's sensory labs, for instance, perfect carbonation's addictive fizz. You're not being tricked. You're being conditioned. Not through coercion, but through repetition. Through feeling. Through reward. These sensory loops set the stage for systems that funnel behavior outright.

III. Designed for Obedience

What looks like convenience is often a behavioral funnel. Clean design, like Netflix's seamless auto-play, removes choices. Subscription models remove exits. Sealed hardware removes alternatives. Auto-renewal removes decision points. Auto-renewal doesn't just remove decision points. It locks in profit. You don't see the fence. You just stay inside it. Everything becomes a closed loop: product to habit to payment to repetition. Resistance requires friction. But friction has been engineered out. You're free to cancel. But you won't. Because the system is too smooth.

IV. Control by Erosion

Control doesn't always arrive as force. Sometimes it arrives as decay. Planned obsolescence doesn't kill products. It wears them out. Not all at once, but piece by piece. Just enough to trigger an upgrade. Just enough to wear down your resistance. Unless resisted, ownership fades into rental. Capability fades into subscription. Repair fades into replacement. Your choices aren't disrupted. They're managed. When Apple throttled iPhones, the company explained it as a way to protect battery life. What was essentially a form of degradation was reframed as a feature.

That's engineered decay. That's behavioral control masked as product care. Control doesn't just erode products. It shapes the spaces you inhabit.

V. The Architecture of Hostility

Even physical space participates. Modern benches are built with bars to prevent lying down. Waiting areas are designed for flow, not comfort. Glass walls, cameras, and passive lighting all serve as signals that you are being watched, directed, and catalogued.

This is not just about security. It is a posture designed to exclude and control. London's anti-homeless benches, for example, aren't safety features. They're containment. You don't need to be told to move along. You'll feel it. You're nudged to obey.

VI. Learned Helplessness, Marketed as Convenience

When most systems are subscription-based, modular, gated, and non-repairable, the limits stop feeling imposed and start feeling natural. You stop asking if things should be this way and start asking which plan fits your budget. You don't question Netflix's grip; you just choose ad-free over basic. You don't repair your iPhone; you trade it in. You do not question the loop because it still works, right up until the moment it fails. You optimize inside a rented life. They call it flexibility. They market it as choice. But it isn't. It's containment. What they sell as ease is structured surrender. People complain on social media about subscription traps, then auto-renew anyway. You live inside a behavioral fence, conditioned not to see it and trained never to shake it.

VII. If You Can't See the Fence, You're Inside It

The brilliance of micro-control is that it doesn't need guards. It needs defaults. It needs smooth UX. It needs recurring billing. It needs your learned routines and divided attention. It thrives on autopilot. Most don't rebel against what they don't notice. Most don't resist what feels normal. That's the architecture. That's the fence. Not to block you from leaving but rather to make sure most never think to try. They claim UX improves lives. But it just tightens the fence.

Compliance Scripts: How Systems Write You Before You Act

The hidden unity behind the mechanisms of engineered identity

I. You Weren't Asked—You Were Formed

You don't wake up and choose a role. You inherit one. Before you speak, you've been categorized. Before you work, you've been filtered. For most people, behavior is shaped long before they understand the system shaping it. Credit scores, gamified platforms, loyalty apps, employer values, corporate pride, wellness trends don't just guide action. They shape identity. Not overtly, but structurally. Not through force, but through reward, omission, and scripted comfort.

II. From Metrics to Morals

A metric is supposed to measure. These systems redefine it to discipline. Credit scores do not simply track repayment. They turn debt into a moral judgment. FICO's "good credit" framing turns lifelong interest payments into proof of character. TikTok's FYP feeds content that affirms your assigned identity. Equifax punishes deviation from financial loyalty. Goop's supplements promise worthiness disguised as health. Even branding becomes a test of alignment. The result isn't neutral measurement. It's value formation. Systems claim meritocracy, but primarily script compliance. You're not just navigating rules. You're internalizing values disguised as benchmarks.

III. Personalization Is Social Control at Scale

Every system calls itself tailored. Customized. Personal. But it's not built for you. They're built to sort you. Netflix's recommendations, like TikTok's FYP, often funnel you into predictable lanes. Spotify's playlists may reflect taste, but the deeper pattern is categorization. You are shown what keeps you from straying, whether politically, behaviorally, or economically. This form of control does not simply categorize. It trains you without giving explicit orders.

Personalization is typically compliance, not individualization. It doesn't reflect who you are. It instructs you on who to become.

IV. Obedience Without a Command

Power no longer speaks in threats. It speaks in interfaces, notifications, likes, and sudden invisibility. You don't need a boss or a priest to enforce behavior. A platform prompt will do. You modify your voice to preserve engagement. You censor yourself to keep reach. You perform your identity in order to avoid drift. You adapt over time, even when you use ad blockers or opt out of personalization, until the system no longer needs to ask. The nudges begin to resemble those found in workplace monitoring apps. You do not feel restricted. You feel optimized.

V. Resistance Looks Like Failure

These systems don't just reward participation. They punish refusal. Not visibly. Quietly. Drop off a social media platform, and your followers vanish. Pay off your credit card, and your score tanks. Skip a wellness app's streak, and the algorithm buries you. On social media, users lament app drop-offs as "failing the system," per 2024 posts. You feel broken, not defiant. The punishment is subtle but cumulative. You stop resisting not because you were defeated but because you were labeled defective.

VI. A System That Writes You in Advance

You are not evaluated for what you've done. You are molded to do what the system expects. These platforms, scores, routines, and rituals don't wait for misbehavior, they enforce preemptive alignment. Preemptive fencing mirrors WEF's 2023 behavioral frameworks, scripting compliance for elites through algorithms, incentives, and "trust indicators." Before you act, you're already sorted. Before you speak, you've already been profiled. And over time, the line between who you are and what the system wants you to be disappears.

Credit Scores as Behavioral Scaffolding

How a Number You Didn't Choose Became the Key to Housing, Work, Insurance, and Obedience

I. The Number You're Taught to Fear

While credit scores are framed as financial risk metrics, they function increasingly as behavioral grading systems. Most people don't fully understand how they work. They just know they're supposed to have a good one. The score blends financial history with behavioral expectations, often rewarding conformity over stability. It punishes you for being unpredictable. That might mean missing a payment, opening accounts irregularly, or straying from expected usage patterns. A credit score doesn't reward independence. It rewards integration.

II. Fiscal Responsibility as Debt Behavior

The system evaluates fiscal responsibility only insofar as it ensures sustained debt. People who avoid credit cards and pay with cash are labeled "thin file" or "credit invisible." They are penalized not for failing to pay, but for failing to participate. This isn't a neutral system. It's a conditioning system. The punishment-reward structure is not only financial. It also operates on a psychological level. It doesn't teach responsibility. It teaches compliance.

III. The Debt Relationship as Identity

Credit scores incentivize a near-permanent relationship with financial institutions. You're rewarded for rotating balances and paying interest. You're penalized for closing accounts or paying debt off too quickly. You are not trusted until you owe something. And not just once. Continuously. Credit scores feed into a broader debt trap, from credit cards to Buy Now, Pay Later schemes, all structured to keep you paying continuously. Debt traps, like subscriptions, make you rent your financial life. It's not about what you can afford. It's about what you owe.

IV. Hacking the Score Isn't Beating It

The culture around credit scores reinforces the trap. People don't question the rules. They swap tips on how to game them. Open a card. Set a $5 autopay. Rotate small charges. Keep your utilization under 10%. Rotating balances to boost scores, for example, racks up interest, enriching banks while you chase a number. These aren't strategies for freedom. They're rituals of obedience dressed up as empowerment. On social media, users boast about hitting 800, unaware they're celebrating a rigged game. They curse landlords checking scores, yet keep borrowing to comply. Score hacking mimics gamified loyalty by rewarding banks, not players. Banks say you choose to play the game. But the rules leave no option.

V. One Number, All Access

This game doesn't stay in your wallet. Employers check credit. Landlords check credit. Insurers and telecom companies check credit. Some dating platforms, like Score, incorporate it. The number increasingly governs access to housing, healthcare, employment, mobility, and even intimacy, despite some resistance, such as California's ban on employer credit checks. Banks claim it levels the playing field. But it penalizes the poor and debt-free alike. It's not just a score. It's a behavioral leash.

VI. No Debate, No Vote, Just Obedience

Credit scores are not required by law. No one voted for them. There is no public oversight. Yet they govern access to essential services. They are private infrastructure embedded in public life. Regulators, complicit in their silence, did little when Equifax's 2017 breach exposed the personal data of 147 million people. Like workplace trackers, credit scores thrive on regulatory neglect. The industry calls this "financial health," "trustworthiness," or "opportunity." But what they reward is obedience.

VII. Compliance Disguised as Legibility

You are not being measured. You are being shaped. The score teaches you to stay in debt, to borrow predictably, to interface with lenders the way they prefer. That isn't assessment. That's scaffolding. And if you grow up inside it, you stop noticing the frame.

VIII. The Score as a Gatekeeper for Movement

A poor credit score doesn't just block access to homes or jobs. It blocks motion. Renting a car without a credit card is nearly impossible. Leasing or financing a vehicle means predatory interest rates or total rejection. Some rideshare apps quietly incorporate credit-linked verification through third-party payment systems. The score isn't just a background check. It's a passcard. When the number is wrong, the system locks you in place.

Credit scores don't just restrict lifestyle, they restrict response. In emergencies, when people need to leave abusive homes, relocate for safety, or access crisis services, poor credit acts as a second barrier. You may qualify for aid or shelter, but not for the rental, the vehicle, or the phone plan needed to reach it. In a society where movement depends on financial trust, a low score can quietly criminalize poverty. It's not just a gauge. It's a restraint system.

IX. Credit Reporting as Private Surveillance

Credit bureaus are not consumer advocates. They are surveillance firms. They monitor your borrowing habits, catalog your payment history, and trade in your behavioral profile. The data you didn't authorize them to collect is bought, sold, and scraped by hedge funds, employers, and insurers. Most people couldn't name the three major bureaus. Even fewer people realize that they are assigned shadow scores, which are estimates of risk and reliability, even if they have not applied for anything.

It's not just your debt that's being tracked. It's your predictability.

X. Generational Entrapment and Normalization

Older generations never had to perform for their credit score. They lived in a world where the number existed, but you didn't have to see it. Many Gen Z users check it weekly. Apps gamify the score with colorful dashboards, swipe prompts, confetti. Creditworthiness becomes a performance. And if you cannot reach a score of 700, you are not simply viewed as irresponsible. You are treated as invisible. What began as a risk metric has become a personality trait. Young people aren't just judged by their number. They internalize it. They start to believe it.

Gamified credit apps don't just nudge behavior. They reshape identity. Many apps now issue progress badges, push celebratory notifications, and offer "challenges" to unlock score improvements. These mechanisms borrow directly from mobile game psychology: variable rewards, status signals, and constant feedback loops. The goal isn't financial literacy. It's behavioral reinforcement. Like a game that rewards you for logging in, the credit system trains users to treat debt activity as self-worth. Compliance becomes play. And play becomes routine.

XI. The Score You Can't See

You're told to maintain a good credit score. But in many cases, you're not even allowed to see it. Federal law grants access to a credit report once a year, but not to your actual score. That's separate. That's a product. For millions of low-income consumers, there is no free dashboard, no credit card that shows the number. They're expected to meet a standard they're not allowed to observe. Imagine taking a test where you never see your grade, only the consequences. That's the system.

XII. Credit as Structural Discrimination

The credit score is race-neutral on its surface. But poverty isn't. And poverty is what it measures. Black and Latino households are more likely to be unbanked, underbanked, and reliant on cash. They are more likely to live in financial systems that penalize them for non-participation. The score doesn't record discrimination directly. It encodes it through patterns: fewer cards, fewer assets, more missed payments, no guarantors. The system doesn't need to know your race. It can read your context.

XIII. The Rise of Credit Vectors

In some corners of the financial industry, the old score is already dying. It's being replaced by something worse. Credit vectors are composite behavioral profiles that gather data from a wide range of sources. These include not only loans and debt, but also rent payments, subscription activity, GPS location, social media behavior, bank app usage, and even how often you charge your phone. These models aren't regulated. They're not disclosed. They don't tell you what's being measured or what weight it carries. You can't contest the result. You may not even know you've been scored.

XIV. The Compliance Spiral

The worse your score, the more expensive your life becomes. High-interest loans. Prepaid phones. Deposit-heavy rentals. Every workaround extracts more from the people who can afford it least. This feedback loop ensures that once you drop below the threshold, it's harder to climb back out. A system designed for risk prediction becomes a mechanism for risk production. Not because it fails but because it works exactly as intended.

The psychological toll of credit pressure is rarely discussed, but profound. Studies link poor credit with higher rates of anxiety, depression, and even suicidal ideation. The feedback loop is vicious: debt worsens mental health, which undermines employment, which deepens financial instability. Yet credit scoring models account for none of this. They reward stability while ignoring the structural causes of instability. The result is a system that punishes the symptoms of stress while profiting from its existence.

Consumer Debt as a Behavioral Leash

How Borrowing Becomes a Tool for Compliance, Not Opportunity

I. Freedom Bought on Credit Isn't Free

Consumer debt is marketed as empowerment. Credit cards promise freedom. Loans promise access. Buy now, pay later schemes promise flexibility. But these are not tools of liberation. They are instruments of control. While debt can provide access, it often does so in a way that constrains long-term autonomy. It doesn't elevate the borrower. It binds them to the lender. Lenders claim debt empowers, but what it buys is obedience.

II. Debt Creates Obedience Without a Badge

A uniform or a time clock is not necessary to enforce submission. Debt performs that role invisibly. A mortgage can turn a homeowner into a neighborhood enforcer, monitoring HOA violations in order to protect property values. A student loan can turn a college dropout into a lifelong wage chaser. A credit card balance can turn a customer into a repeat buyer, afraid to default and unable to pause. The debtor does not need surveillance. They monitor themselves.

III. Monthly Payments as Behavioral Infrastructure

A consumer with fixed monthly payments, including rent, car loans, insurance, phone bills, and credit card debt, is less likely to strike, less likely to quit, and less likely to dissent. Every installment acts as a leash. Every due date serves as a checkpoint.

Debt transforms unpredictable people into stable revenue streams. They are no longer treated as citizens or workers. They are managed as accounts.

IV. Debt as a Gatekeeping Credential

In the credit score chapter, we saw how debt history becomes an identity credential. Here, the debt itself becomes the filter. You can't rent without a deposit. You can't get a deposit without a card. You can't get a card without a job. And you can't keep the job if the card debt gets too high. It's not a vicious cycle. It's a closed loop. A system designed to turn instability into compliance. This closed loop doesn't just gatekeep. It rebrands dependence as maturity.

V. Emotional Branding of Personal Finance

Financial literacy campaigns warn against bad debt but teach management, not resistance. Responsibility is framed not as independence from credit, but as disciplined, ongoing participation in it. Good debt. Strategic debt. Smart borrowing. The language is moral, not mathematical. It's not about APR. It's about character. Like corporate feminism, financial literacy masks control as progress.

VI. Interest as Institutional Extraction

The logic of interest is not neutral. It is designed to make the lender rich without producing anything. A $1,000 balance at 24% interest earns the bank more than a thousand-dollar product ever could. Debt is the only product that grows by being unfulfilled. The borrower stays stuck. The balance stays alive. The profit stays passive. Interest extraction mirrors the IMF's playbook of growth through debt, not output.

VII. Debt as a Condition of Participation

For most, to opt out of consumer debt is to opt out of modern life. No credit? No apartment. No car. No phone plan. No airline ticket. Debt isn't an emergency solution. It's the default setting. If you're not borrowing, you're not counted. The system calls this inclusion. What it means is: you're either paying, or you're locked out.

VIII. Normalization of Indebtedness

Once, being in debt was a crisis. Now, it's a lifestyle. The average American carries nearly four credit cards and carries about $6,500 in balances, contributing to a national debt total of $1.2 trillion. This is not an exception. It is the norm. "Zero down" offers, "pay over time" checkout options, and "easy monthly installments" are now routine. Debt is no longer treated as a symptom of poverty. It has become the model for participating in middle-class life.

IX. Financialized Compliance

Debt changes how people behave and not just toward lenders, but toward each other. Roommates tolerate abuse to avoid breaking leases. Workers endure exploitation to keep health coverage. A 2023 study found 40% of couples cite debt stress as a reason to stay in strained marriages. The more enmeshed your debts, the harder it is for many to move. To act. To say no. This compliance doesn't just bind individuals, it shapes futures.

X. Student Debt as Future Discipline

Student debt is not just a burden. It's a behavioral regulator. It influences what people major in, where they live, who they marry, how they vote. It delays risk. It discourages dissent. It turns education into a financial bet and turns the student into a risk-averse investor in their own restraint. Brookings (2023) found student debt steers students toward STEM and blue states, curbing instability. What's sold as knowledge becomes a contract of control.

XI. Buy Now Pay Later as Psychological Training

BNPL schemes like Klarna and Affirm are not about affordability. They are about habituation. Teaching young consumers to split a $40 hoodie into four payments isn't convenience. It's priming. It's the soft launch of chronic debt. Klarna's rates, up to 25%, rival credit cards, turning trinkets into debt traps. Like subscriptions, BNPL rents your spending. Like Fortnite's microtransactions, BNPL gamifies consumption. On social media, users curse Klarna's traps yet keep splitting payments.

XII. Language of Delay, System of Dependence

The debt industry rarely uses the word "debt." It uses terms like financing, pre-approval, membership, credit line, delayed billing, and flexible options. These phrases are designed to reframe obligation as opportunity and to make borrowing feel like a benefit rather than a burden.

But behind every euphemism is the same mechanism: you get it now, and pay more later. It's not flexibility. It's acceleration of consumption and deferral of pain. The more urgent the desire, the easier the capture.

XIII. Debt and Class Performance

Debt allows working-class consumers to simulate middle-class life. That's the trick. You look stable while you sink. You have the shoes, the couch, the car, and the phone, but you do not have the cushion. The image of security is bought on borrowed time. The interest paid to preserve that image is the price of performance.

XIV. The Leash Tightens in Private

Debt does not announce itself loudly. It operates quietly, shaping behavior through small, cumulative pressures. A missed payment here, a declined charge there, and gradually the boundaries of what feels possible begin to narrow. It teaches restraint without commands, warning you not to dream too ambitiously, move too quickly, or take risks that might jeopardize stability. There is no need for a supervisor to shout or a court to impose punishment. The correction happens internally. Over time, the restraints are no longer external at all. The leash is not visible, because it is made of habits. Once those habits become routine, they are nearly impossible to recognize, let alone escape.

Where debt engineers obedience through necessity, gamified systems offer rewards that feel like agency, even when they reinforce the same behavioral limits.

Gamification and Loyalty Loops

How Point Systems, Badges, and Behavioral Rewards Train You to Serve Invisible Agendas

I. When the Game Isn't a Game

Gamification is not about fun. It's about control. The term sounds harmless. It describes game design applied to non-game settings. But its purpose is not enjoyment. Its purpose is obedience. It attaches reward triggers to real-world behavior. You get points for actions. Badges for habits. Leaderboards for consistency. It makes compliance feel like achievement. While gamified systems can encourage habit formation and learning, they are increasingly optimized for extraction rather than enrichment.

II. Loyalty by Design, Not Choice

Loyalty programs don't measure loyalty. They manufacture it. Airline miles, coffee stamps, punch cards, and app streaks create sunk costs, not relationships. Once you start collecting, you don't want to stop. You fly Delta to keep SkyMiles, even if United's cheaper, because abandoning points feels like loss. The original goal may be convenience, personal preference, or user satisfaction, but it is eventually replaced by the system's true objective: repeat engagement.

III. Variable Rewards and Operant Traps

Gamified systems rely on intermittent reinforcement, the same structure used in slot machines. Many platforms use variable rewards to drive engagement, even when those rewards offer little or no intrinsic value. The reward frequency changes, but the action stays the same. It teaches persistence without reflection. If a system trains you to try again regardless of outcome, you're not playing. You're being conditioned.

IV. Progress Bars as Leashes

Progress bars turn goals into obligations. Once you're 70% through a challenge or reward cycle, quitting feels like failure. Apps and brands use this psychology deliberately. Finish your week. Maintain your streak. You've almost earned your next rank. What began as a neutral tracker becomes a behavioral tether forever nudging you forward even when you want to stop. On social media, users celebrate Duolingo streaks but also lament the pressure to stay locked in.

V. Gamification as Surveillance Incentive

Fitness apps gamify steps and sleep, but they also harvest biometric and location data. Language apps gamify usage streaks while collecting audio samples and user behavior logs. The more you play, the more data they collect, whether for improving features or for surveillance purposes. Fitbit's 2021 Google acquisition raised data-sharing concerns. These aren't just engagement platforms. They're biometric funnels feeding ad networks, insurers, and corporate surveillance systems. Like health apps, fitness trackers sell data to insurers and monetize compliance.

VI. The Illusion of Agency

Gamification systems present themselves as tools for self-improvement. They invite you to track your habits, measure progress, and level up your life. But beneath the surface, these structures are designed to reroute behavior. Health apps may lead to better fitness, but their primary function is to sustain engagement. What appears to be goal-setting is often a reaction to prompts. What feels like progress is the completion of tasks designed by someone else. The goals are not your own. Apps that claim to empower are built to redirect your attention, shape your routines, and monetize your effort.

VII. Digital Labor Without Compensation

Gamified systems often extract labor without acknowledging it. Google Maps gamifies location feedback. Waze crowdsources traffic reports from unpaid drivers. Fitness apps sell aggregated movement data to insurers. Duolingo once relied on millions of unpaid translators; now it harvests user behavior to train AI. When the reward is a badge or a rank, it's easier to forget that you're doing free work for someone else's profit.

VIII. Loyalty to the Interface, Not the Brand

Gamification doesn't build loyalty to a product. It builds loyalty to a loop. You don't stick with one airline because it's good. You stick because your miles are trapped there. You don't keep ordering from the same app because it's better. You keep going to maintain your streak. The reward structure overrides all other evaluation. The more points you collect, the more power the system has over most users, unless you break free.

IX. Gamification as Distraction Architecture

Gamified interfaces obscure the core transaction. Ride apps do not display pricing in a straightforward way. Instead, they highlight "badges unlocked." Health insurance apps rarely explain policy terms clearly. Instead, they focus on showing "daily wins." Apps prioritize engagement over clarity, using metrics to distract from real costs. Like corporate feminism, gamified apps mask exploitation with wins. Every swipe, every tap, every "daily check-in" replaces scrutiny with autopilot compliance.

X. Points and Paywalls

Points, ranks, and credits replace money in many gamified systems. This substitution isn't accidental. Points feel lighter than dollars. They create artificial economies where the rules can change, the value can drop, and the user has no recourse. Premium tiers and in-app purchases are inserted where progress stalls. Fortnite's microtransactions gate progress the same way premium apps do. What begins as a free tool becomes a gated loop. Like credit vectors, these systems use opaque metrics to extract payment. Like subscriptions, paywalls rent your engagement. Like planned obsolescence, they engineer decay in your wallet.

XI. Education, But Addictive

Gamification has spread to schools. Students earn stars for homework, streaks for attendance, coins for quiz completion. Behavior is rewarded with badges, not understanding. Attention is trained on metrics, not meaning. ClassDojo, for example, trains students to accumulate points, not curiosity. A 2022 study found ClassDojo's points fade post-game, prioritizing compliance over learning. The system doesn't build intellect. It builds obedience.

XII. When Loss Feels Like Failure

Gamification systems are not passive. They use loss aversion to increase dependence. If you miss a day, your streak resets. If you change services, your points vanish. These systems turn neutrality into punishment. Missing a goal isn't just nothing. It becomes a loss. And that loss is designed to feel personal, not arbitrary. On social media, users mourn reset streaks, describing guilt, frustration, and failure over what should be a neutral outcome.

XIII. Who Designs the Game?

Gamification feels modern, but the logic is ancient: reward obedience, punish deviation, obscure authorship. The real question isn't how the system works. It's who benefits when you play. Every game has a designer. And in the modern loyalty loop, the user is never one of them.

What apps achieve through points and prompts, belief systems accomplish through sacred routines. Both reinforce identity through repetition, not reflection

Religion and Wellness as Identity Scripts

How Systems of Faith and Self-Care Shape Behavior Through Ritual and Belonging

I. Faith Systems Don't Just Comfort—They Conform

Religion has always been a tool for shaping identity. Not just beliefs, but behaviors. Not just rituals, but boundaries. It tells you who you are, what to do, how to live, and, most importantly, how to judge others. It organizes thought into morality. It turns obedience into virtue. And once it is internalized, it no longer needs enforcement. It becomes the lens through which life is interpreted. Catholic confession, for example, turns guilt into obedience by privatizing judgment and reinforcing identity.

II. Morality as a Preset

In many religious systems, morality is often received, not reasoned. Sin isn't defined by consequence. It's defined by deviation. The ritual isn't functional. It's formative. You do the thing not because it works, but because it's commanded. Right and wrong are typically separated from context. The script trains you to accept answers before asking questions.

III. The Narrative of Redemption Through Suffering

Most institutional religions romanticize suffering. Christianity's "carry your cross" frames struggle as sacred, pain as purification, endurance as divine. This narrative isn't neutral. It discourages revolt. It glorifies submission. The one who suffers and obeys is rewarded later. Not here. Not now. Later. Which makes it easier to justify injustice as spiritually productive.

IV. Ritual as Identity

Rituals aren't just sacred. They are also anchoring. Whether it's Catholic Mass, Islamic prayer, or Evangelical tithing, rituals create rhythm, predictability, and certainty. But they also establish checkpoints of belonging. Are you performing correctly? Are you doing enough? Evangelical tithing tracks devotion, like wellness apps track steps. Skipping one becomes a red flag. The ritual isn't for the divine, it's also for the group.

V. Surveillance by Community

Religious institutions don't need CCTV. They have each other. Gossip. Guilt. Mutual observation. A decentralized enforcement network. Everyone watches everyone else for deviation. In rigid communities, suspicion often knows no limits, even within inclusive faiths such as Unitarianism or progressive religious circles. Thought crimes are judged by tone, absence, doubt. This isn't spirituality. It's social compliance wrapped in theology.

VI. Belief as Brand Loyalty

Belief systems sell identity in total. You don't just believe a creed. You wear it, post it, affirm it socially. You adopt the language, the attire, and the cultural signifiers. It becomes a brand: cohesive, performative, recognizable. And like any brand, deviation is punished by exclusion. This brand loyalty doesn't just bind. It's repackaged as wellness.

VII. Enter Wellness

Wellness is marketed as the secular replacement for faith. Not necessarily a belief in the divine, but a belief in transformation. It presents itself as a lifestyle, a journey, a set of personal practices. But its architecture is familiar: fixed precepts, repetitive rituals, binaries of clean versus toxic, and a moralized vision of success. Like religion, it offers belonging through adherence. Like corporate wellness, it demands continual adaptation. This isn't just self-care. It's a belief system. And like any belief system, it imposes rules that are often unspoken, but always enforced.

VIII. The Wellness Moral Code

The wellness world does more than offer routines; it delivers a moral framework. Eat this, not that. Meditate daily. Breathe with intention. Journal your mindset. Buy organic. Avoid seed oils. Wake up early. Practice cold exposure. Each recommendation is more than a health suggestion. It is a behavioral expectation. The products and practices marketed by companies like Goop, from supplements to self-care regimens, imply that vitality is not merely attainable, but deserved through purchase. As the rituals accumulate and the expectations multiply, noncompliance begins to feel like a personal failing rather than a reasonable boundary. Fatigue is no longer just a symptom. It becomes evidence that you are misaligned. And in a culture that treats optimization as moral worth, failure to keep up is no longer neutral. It becomes an indictment of character.

IX. Optimization as Salvation

Where religion promises spiritual growth, wellness promises peak selfhood. You'll be more focused. More productive. More beautiful. More energized. The vision is not enlightenment. It's another performance. The body becomes the altar. Discipline becomes faith. The goal isn't peace. It's improvement without end. Wellness claims to empower but it scripts compliance.

X. Rituals for the Algorithm

Wellness rituals are now public, posted, tracked, and monetized. Influencers perform their routines not as testimony but as advertising. The prayer mat is replaced by the camera lens. The devotional is replaced by the morning stack. On X, users share #SelfCare fails, lamenting fatigue as shame, chasing engagement. The ritual doesn't stay private. It becomes content.

XI. Shame as Social Regulation

Failure to thrive becomes shameful. Depression becomes a branding problem. Fatigue becomes a mindset flaw. Wellness culture primarily places the blame for failure on the individual, even while it acknowledges the presence of systemic stress. On social media, users confess wellness fails as shame, not struggle. Like sin, unwellness becomes internalized as a moral defect. Not a product of context. A failure of self. This shame does more than regulate behavior. It is amplified by algorithms.

XII. Conversion by Algorithm

Wellness culture spreads not through missionaries but through platforms. Your feed learns what you want. Then it teaches you what to fear. Then it sells you the solution. TikTok's FYP pushes $50 collagen for "tired skin," fueling consumption. Each product implies a deficiency. Each routine implies a void. You don't explore wellness. You are shown it. And once shown, you are shown again.

XIII. The Altar of Optimization

Wellness replaces the divine with the optimized. Instead of obeying God, you obey the version of yourself you haven't reached yet. You invest your time, your money, your attention in the hopes of becoming someone you already suspect isn't real. Optimization echoes WEF's "human capital" rhetoric. The gospel isn't transcendence. It's control through aspiration.

XIV. Identity by Subscription

Religion was once weekly. Wellness is hourly. Each scroll, each product, each practice is another reminder of who you're supposed to be. It doesn't demand belief. It demands maintenance. And when that maintenance becomes a lifestyle, and that lifestyle becomes your identity, you're no longer choosing. You're performing. The script isn't just running. It's a script you can't unsubscribe.

Work-Life Balance as Corporate Myth

How the Promise of Harmony Became a Tool of Compliance

I. Balance Was Never the Goal

"Work-life balance" sounds like fairness. A measured scale. A personal achievement. But it's not a policy. It's a slogan. No one defines it. No one enforces it. It's a moving target that shifts with burnout, deadlines, and economic fear. It's not a system of protection. It's a performance metric for self-management.

II. The Myth That You Control the Scale

"Balance" implies that imbalance is your fault. You didn't prioritize. You didn't set boundaries. You failed to say no. But for most workers, the demand is structural. With median rent at $1,500 and half of Americans tied to employer insurance, boundaries are a myth. You don't choose burnout. You adjust to it.

III. Flexibility as a Smokescreen

Employers offer flexibility to look humane. But flexibility almost always flows one way. You can leave early if you answer emails at night. You can work from home if you're always available. You can take a sick day if you never actually use it. Firms claim you choose flexibility, but it's one-directional. The trade is clear: visible labor shrinks, invisible labor expands.

IV. Wellness as a Liability Shield

Workplaces now offer wellness apps, yoga sessions, and

meditation exercises as tools to address stress. But these resources are not designed as safety nets. They function as instruments of risk management. A burned-out employee who leaves the job creates cost. A worker who journals through mistreatment, on the other hand, remains productive. Apps like Calm, promoted by companies such as Amazon, offer a space to vent, but only in ways that allow productivity to continue without interruption. On social media, users often mock corporate-sponsored wellness tools like yoga apps, yet many still engage with them. This version of wellness does not offer protection. It simply demands a more polished form of endurance.

V. The Performance of Balance

Workers today face pressure not only to meet expectations, but to appear composed while doing it. You are expected to perform at a high level and simultaneously make it seem as if the effort comes at no personal cost. In meetings, you maintain a calm demeanor. Online, you express gratitude and enthusiasm. Projecting the image of thriving has become part of the job itself. The stress does not come only from the workload. It also comes from the constant demand to hide its impact. Managers may ask how you are feeling, but Employee Assistance Programs rarely lead to reduced responsibilities. The result is not care. It is a performance of empathy that substitutes optics for real change.

VI. The Always-On Economy

Phones erased the boundaries of the workday. Apps blurred the lines of the weekend. Notifications disrupted the ability to disconnect. Workers now live in a state of constant partial engagement. They must always be reachable, but are rarely fully present. Time is no longer clearly divided. It has become fragmented, and each fragment holds potential for monetization. Even with digital detox efforts, notifications continue to rent slices of your attention. Like subscription models, they turn presence into a recurring charge.

VII. Self-Care as Internalized Responsibility

The more the system wears you down, the more you are encouraged to manage the exhaustion on your own. Feeling burned out? Try meditation. Struggling with depression? Go for a walk. Facing a crisis? Step away from your screen. The message is not to change the system but to adjust yourself to its demands without resistance. What were once seen as institutional failures are now rebranded as personal challenges in resilience.

VIII. Gig Work and the Disappearance of Time

In the gig economy, time is no longer something workers schedule. It is something they scrape together. Uber's algorithm pushes drivers to chase surge pricing, transforming each hour into a gamble rather than a guarantee. DoorDash's pay structure locks workers into extended shifts, with earnings targets that shift unpredictably as they try to reach them. There is no defined shift. There is no clear end. Every waking hour becomes either a potential opportunity or a looming financial risk.

IX. The Optics of Empathy

Human resources departments now track burnout. Managers ask about wellness. But when conditions remain unchanged, these gestures do not reflect care. They function as compliance theater. Phrases like "How are you feeling?" become scripted checkpoints rather than genuine attempts to address underlying issues. Wellness goals are folded into performance reviews, turning the appearance of empathy into a measurable metric. Much like distraction architecture in app design, the system offers the illusion of concern while continuing to impose the same expectations and demands.

X. Time Off as a Threat

In workplaces that glorify grind, vacation becomes a risk. Take your time, and you signal disloyalty. Don't take it, and you burn out. Either way, the system wins. Unlimited PTO sounds generous. But it also means no accrual, no payout, and no accountability. A 2022 study found workers with unlimited PTO take less time, fearing disloyalty or judgment. What looks like freedom is a bookkeeping trick.

XI. Career Framing as Moral Growth

Work is now marketed as a personal journey that should be driven by passion, and it's framed as a calling. Jobs are no longer presented as tasks to complete, but as opportunities for self-growth and identity formation. Apple's "think different" campaign, for example, casts work as a reflection of who you are. In this framework, quitting can feel like betrayal, not of the company, but of the self. The job is no longer just labor. It becomes a mirror. And the ideal worker is the one who believes that the reflection it shows is who they truly are.

XII. Balance as Branding

Companies use "balance" to describe their culture. Not their expectations. Ping pong tables, coffee bars, quiet rooms, and the optics of peace replace the policies of rest. The image of a balanced life becomes a recruiting tool. And once you're inside, the balance disappears. Like corporate feminism, balance branding masks exploitation as progress. Like the WEF's "future of work" rhetoric, it sells exhaustion as transformation.

XIII. The Fantasy of Control

The idea of "balance" suggests a clear set of options: work more or rest more, spend time here or there. But for most workers, these choices are not equal. The real decision is often not between balance and freedom, but between exhaustion and economic instability. The language of balance obscures the deeper issue: a lack of power. There is no balance when you are the one holding up both sides.

XIV. Nothing Is Off the Clock

Work-life balance fails not because people mismanage time, but because the system doesn't recognize a boundary. Hustle is monetized. Passion is extracted. Rest is borrowed against future output. If your presence is a profit source, your absence becomes a cost. And when your rest becomes debt, you don't recover. You owe.

Even as the workplace scripts behavior through the illusion of balance, the world outside the office offers no real relief. What appears to be rebellion often mirrors the same structures it claims to resist. Branded dissent, curated rage, and corporate-sponsored movements promise empowerment but deliver performance. What once signaled resistance is now designed to showcase alignment.

Manufactured Movements

How Corporate Feminism and Brand Activism Reframe Control as Empowerment

I. Resistance Becomes a Marketing Tool

When a corporation says it supports a movement, it often means it supports the performance of support. Social justice has been rebranded as a marketing asset. Solidarity is reduced to a slogan. Liberation is reframed as a lifestyle product. The message shifts from "fight the system" to "shop with us."

II. Corporate Feminism Isn't Feminism

Feminism that begins and ends with a boardroom promotion cannot be called feminism. It is a corporate incentive structure dressed in pink branding. Empowerment is redefined as salary. Strength is reduced to a job title. Equity is repackaged as a marketing tagline. Nike's "Dream Crazier" campaign, for example, frames empowerment as a matter of buying sneakers rather than addressing systemic barriers. These campaigns draw from the language of liberation but remain comfortably aligned with the structures they claim to challenge.

III. Representation Without Redistribution

The faces on the website change. The voices in the commercial shift. But the structure remains. You can diversify a cabinet without changing the policy. You can diversify a board without changing the company's behavior. Representation is visibility and rarely transformation. Firms claim DEI drives change, but it usually decorates power, not redistributes it.

IV. Logos at the Protest, Ads in the Feed

Corporations now absorb and repackage the symbols of rebellion. Rainbow logos are displayed during Pride Month. Raised fists appear in campaigns referencing Black Lives Matter. Hashtags that once conveyed urgency have been folded into brand identity. What once served to disrupt now functions as a tool for directing attention and generating engagement. On social media, users often describe Target's Pride merchandise as a cash grab, yet many still make the purchase. The protest is not erased. It is sold.

V. The Safe Rebellion

Manufactured movements provide the sensation of resistance without exposing participants to its consequences. You purchase the shirt, share the square, and nod in agreement with the advertisement. In this dynamic, genuine political risk is replaced with symbolic, aesthetic gestures. What once demanded discomfort, confrontation, and clarity now becomes an easy form of participation. Even when grassroots organizers push back, the broader system continues to appear progressive because it has learned to clothe itself in the visual language of dissent.

VI. Hashtag Empathy, Policy Apathy

Brand activism tends to be loud on Instagram but quiet in legislative halls. Even when the values appear to align, the action often stops at the surface. Public empathy is inexpensive. Structural reform requires real cost. AT&T, for example, promoted Pride-themed content while simultaneously contributing $3 million to Republican campaigns known for supporting anti-

LGBTQ+ policies (OpenSecrets, 2023). This contradiction is not unique. Many companies publicly declare "we care," while financially backing the very systems and political structures they claim to oppose.

VII. Inclusivity as a Gatekeeping Filter

You are now invited to bring your whole self to work but only so long as that self fits the brand. Authenticity is encouraged, but curated. Diversity is welcome, but channeled. Expression is monitored for alignment. Like gamified loyalty apps, inclusivity becomes a filter for behavioral conformity.

VIII. Internal Branding of Identity

Modern workers aren't just expected to perform tasks. You're expected not just to do the job, but to embody the brand. You don't just work at a company, you embody its values. Google's 2022 performance reviews tied bonuses to DEI alignment, enforcing corporate scripts. The company no longer sells a product. It sells itself as a worldview. You become the avatar.

IX. Pride Month Ends at the Loading Dock

A corporation can sponsor a Pride float in the morning and outsource to sweatshops in the afternoon. H&M's 2023 Pride campaign ran alongside reports of wage theft and unsafe labor conditions in Bangladesh (The Guardian, 2023). Brand activism doesn't require consistency. It requires optics and optics don't trick the powerful. They pacify the rest.

X. Corporate Feminism's Real Legacy

The rise of the "girlboss" did not dismantle corporate hierarchies; it simply made them personal. The ladder remained intact but was rebranded as empowerment. When the image collapsed under backlash, the system did not move toward equity; it shifted to more polished messaging. Like work-life balance campaigns, corporate feminism disguises structural harm behind the language of self-improvement.

XI. The Safety of Branded Rage

Rage that once fueled disruption has been redirected into consumption. Express your politics through a purchase. Channel your dissent into merch. On social media, users mock DEI posts for not stopping layoffs, yet repost them anyway. Rage becomes a currency. But the transaction benefits someone else.

XII. From Boycott to Buy-In

Activism used to mean divestment. Now it means emotional investment. You're told to support companies that align with your values. But what values are left when the labor is the same, the product is the same, and the harm is identical? You're not voting with your wallet. You're handing your conscience to the brand.

XIII. The Illusion of Shared Struggle

Corporations now talk like movements. They say "we." They say "together." They borrow the cadence of solidarity while protecting their margins. WEF's stakeholder capitalism narrative mirrors this tone, claiming unity while engineering control. They don't join the struggle. They brand it. And sell it back to you with a markup. While some brands avoid politicized positioning, the trend has tilted toward moral signaling as marketing strategy.

XIV. What Was Once Dangerous Is Now Safe to Print

Decades ago, movements were surveilled. Crushed. Leaders were jailed or killed. Today, those same slogans appear on Walmart tote bags. Not because justice prevailed, but because the threat has been defused. BLM's 2020 demands became merch by 2023 (Vox). The message wasn't embraced. It was flattened. What survives isn't the danger. It's the font.

The systems examined here do not rely on force or prohibition. They shape identity through incentives, rituals, and subtle design. Participation is rewarded, refusal is quietly punished, and the personal is absorbed into infrastructure. Belief, health, values, and even dissent are rendered as behavioral patterns to be monitored and aligned. But identity scripting is only the beginning. The next section shifts from internal formation to external control and from shaping who you are to determining what you are permitted to do.

Education as Behavioral Blueprint

How School Became the First Platform for Identity Compliance

I. Formatting Begins with the Body

The systems that shape identity don't stop at belief. They continue into behavior, deciding not just who you are, but what you're allowed to access. Public education is framed as a moral achievement: equal access to knowledge, civic preparation, and upward mobility. But from its structure to its rituals, it functions less as a tool for liberation than as a behavioral template. Bells segment time into obedient units. Desks are aligned to discourage disruption. Movement is tightly permissioned. Students are taught not only facts, but posture, silence, and symbolic compliance. By age seven, they've been conditioned to ask before peeing. This isn't an accident. It's formatting. What presents as benevolent instruction doubles as early adaptation to bureaucratic control. The school isn't neutral. It's the first operating system (as explored in our analysis of time discipline).

II. Curriculum as Behavioral Script

The content taught in school appears neutral but is shaped by political and economic power. History textbooks omit radical labor movements, resistance campaigns, and systemic critiques. In 2023, Texas revised its history standards to downplay labor strikes and erase César Chávez, framing American progress through corporate innovation and patriotic consensus (Education Week, 2023). Literature curricula strip down novels to vocabulary words and character arcs, removing context and critique. Civics is sanitized: civil rights are framed as completed projects, not ongoing struggles. Even science is reduced to compliance with procedure rather than engagement with uncertainty. Lessons typically reinforce assumptions and often frame the system as orderly, complete, and right. There are exceptions (California's ethnic studies requirement, select International Baccalaureate programs) but these are structurally rare. The average classroom encodes norms, not questions. What students learn is that the system works, and deviation is friction.

III. Obedience as Virtue

Good students are quiet, punctual, and compliant. Disruption is punished, not explored. Students who ask "why" are often labeled difficult. Questioning the purpose of an assignment can result in lowered grades or disciplinary action, even when curiosity drives the inquiry. On social media, students frequently post complaints about being penalized for "talking back" after objecting to unclear or contradictory instructions. A 2024 post reads: "Got detention for asking what the assignment was even about. Guess thinking too hard is a crime now." These aren't isolated gripes. They reflect the normalization of obedience as a moral good. While progressive teachers push back, and student protests occasionally force local reforms (Education Week, 2024), the dominant infrastructure still rewards submission. According to NEA survey data (2023), even educators who value student voice often feel constrained by testing mandates and behavior rubrics. Obedience remains the price of approval, despite mounting resistance.

IV. Tracking as Early Class Stratification

The education system does not distribute opportunity equally. It sorts. From as early as third grade, students are routed into tracks that reflect race, class, and parental education more than potential. Chicago's 2024 gifted and talented placement data revealed a disproportionate skew: students from households earning over $100,000 per year were three times more likely to be identified as "gifted" compared to students from households earning under $40,000 (Chicago Tribune, 2024). Standardized testing, long marketed as objective, reflects disparities in nutrition, trauma exposure, sleep, and access to early enrichment, all of which correlate with socioeconomic status. Once assigned, tracks become destiny. Students in lower tracks receive less rigorous instruction, fewer enrichment opportunities, and more behavioral surveillance. By the time they reach high school, these students often believe they are inherently less capable. The stratification is not diagnostic. It is performative. It teaches children to accept their placement as deserved, even when the data shows it was predicted by zip code.

V. Meritocracy as Ideological Control

Students are taught that effort equals outcome. That if they fail, it's because they didn't try hard enough. This myth persists despite mountains of data to the contrary. In 2024, Detroit's public schools were funded at approximately $9,000 per student, compared to $15,000 per student in nearby suburban districts (EdTrust, 2024). Graduation rates, test scores, and college admissions mirrored the funding gap. Yet the dominant narrative remains: the system is fair, and hard work will be rewarded. When schools fail to deliver equitable outcomes, the blame is redirected onto students, parents, or vague cultural deficits. Some districts, such as those following Montessori or restorative justice frameworks, attempt to disrupt this pattern. But they are the exception, not the rule. Meritocracy primarily functions to neutralize criticism. It tells the underprivileged that their suffering is their fault, and the privileged that their success is earned. The fiction is not accidental. It is ideological armor.

VI. The Classroom as Prototype Workplace

School trains students to inhabit corporate logic long before they enter the workforce. Time is segmented into task blocks. Instructions flow from authority to subordinate. Performance is evaluated impersonally through points and rubrics. Failure is punished, not restructured. Creativity is bounded by template. Collaboration is monitored and graded. Even the physical environment mimics the workplace: fluorescent lights, rigid seating, uniform dress codes. Surveillance is normalized through hall passes, behavioral logs, and increasingly, digital monitoring. This is not preparation for work. It is a soft initiation into labor culture. Students are not asked to create; they are asked to produce. Not to question; but to execute. Schools do not just prepare children for capitalism. They embed its logic in their bones. The bell schedule may have begun with factories (see earlier analysis of time discipline), but its structure now serves knowledge work, surveillance, and algorithmic assessment just as easily.

VII. Choice as Interface Illusion

The modern education system has adapted to critiques by offering "choices": magnet schools, career academies, charter programs, electives. But these choices are pre-structured. A child may choose which path to take, but only from a narrow corridor of state-sanctioned options. Career days do not feature whistleblowers or activists. They feature engineers, nurses, managers. The archetype is not the dissenter; it is the contributor. College admissions have become baroque rituals of conformity. GPA, AP load, volunteer hours, and extracurriculars are metrics that reward bureaucratic mastery, not intellectual depth. In 2025, Common App essays were analyzed for "authentic voice" using AI scoring tools adopted by over 200 colleges. These tools rewarded algorithmically detectable conformity over originality (Inside Higher Ed, 2025). Even self-expression is run through filters. Students are told they're building a future, but the future was chosen before they arrived.

VIII. Internalization as Self-Governance

By the end of their schooling, most students do not resist the system. They replicate it. Future teachers, counselors, administrators, and even critics are pulled from the same pool of students shaped by institutional values. This is the true power of behavioral blueprints: the formatting becomes invisible. You enforce the system because you believe it. You protect it because it feels natural. The World Economic Forum's 2023 *Global Education Futures* report outlines a framework for "resilience-based identity cultivation," a euphemism for shaping compliant workers through "values-forward" schooling. This isn't a conspiracy. It's a blueprint. It was published, promoted, and uncritically adopted by governments and NGOs. The Gates Foundation's long-standing support of Common Core and outcome-based evaluation systems reflects this same ideology: measurement over meaning, optimization over autonomy. The system's durability is not a function of its strength. It is a function of how thoroughly it has been installed inside the minds of those tasked with running it.

Student Loans and the School-to-Debt Pipeline

How Education Converts Aspiration into Leverage

I. The Promise Comes First

From childhood, Americans are taught that higher education is the gateway to opportunity. School counselors, pop culture, and federal policy converge around a single message: go to college, and you'll build a better life. This promise is presented as fact: inevitable, noble, and necessary. By high school, students are scheduling SATs, mapping FAFSA deadlines, and crafting "dream school" lists. College is not framed as optional. It is framed as a moral project: a choice to rise, to grow, to prove worth.

But degrees don't guarantee opportunity. They script debt. In 2024, over 43 million Americans held federal student loans, totaling more than $1.6 trillion (Dept. of Education, 2024). The average undergraduate borrower owed over $29,000 at graduation. Education's value is not measured in learning. It is measured in balance sheets. The promise isn't broken. It is collateralized.

II. Loans as Conditioning Tool

Student loans are not just financing mechanisms. They are behavioral blueprints. The pressure begins before the first class is attended. Borrowers are taught to track balances, monitor interest, and avoid default before they've ever held a salaried job. The stress is immediate and persistent. In 2024, 72% of borrowers reported moderate to severe anxiety linked to their student debt (JAMA, 2024).

Debt stress narrows choice. Students are less likely to switch majors, transfer schools, or take intellectual risks if their debt is mounting. Post-graduation, job decisions become risk-averse. Public service becomes aspirational. Corporate compliance becomes default. For adjunct faculty, earning $3,000 per course in 2024, student loans remain an anchor that ties low-wage academic labor to the same institutions that sold them debt (AAUP, 2024). This is not financing. It is formatting. The loan doesn't just fund the degree. It trains the user.

III. The Illusion of Choice

Borrowers are told they "chose" their loans. But the choice is typically rigged. Most middle-class and low-income families cannot pay tuition out of pocket. Scholarships are scarce, often biased toward high-performing or legacy applicants. FAFSA is mandatory. Federal loans are nearly automatic.
In 2024, 91% of undergraduate students at four-year public universities used some form of financial aid (NCES, 2024). While some students, such as those using military benefits or attending tuition-free institutions, bypass debt, the overwhelming majority do not. Choice often means choosing between loan and exclusion. This resembles the healthcare system's "choice" between coverage tiers. Freedom exists only in the margins. The illusion of choice shields the lender. If the decision was voluntary, the burden is yours. The system, once again, remains blameless.

IV. Interest as Structural Discipline

Interest is not just a fee. It is a behavioral throttle. Borrowers are constantly made aware of their ticking balances. Even in deferment, interest often capitalizes and compounds silently. Take a semester off, choose a fellowship, or face a family emergency, and the penalty is financial. Exploration becomes risky. Stillness becomes safe.

This discipline doesn't just constrain. It dangles false relief. Income-driven repayment plans, used by nearly half of all federal borrowers in 2024, offer lower monthly payments but often extend timelines past 20 years (Dept. of Education, 2024.) These plans resemble other systems of conditional access, like Medicaid, which requires regular proof of compliance to maintain coverage, or hospital software that flags patients based on algorithm-friendly behavior rather than clinical need. You either perform standard behavior or you trigger review. Resistance does exist. Loan strikes, debt cancellation movements, and nonprofit advocacy challenge the structure. Yet the maze often restrains, despite partial waivers or temporary relief efforts. Borrowers remain inside a system designed to offer mercy only through performance.

V. Forgiveness as Containment

Public Service Loan Forgiveness (PSLF) promises cancellation, but only after 120 qualifying payments under perfect paperwork. Change jobs or use the wrong repayment plan, and the clock resets. In 2022, fewer than 5% of PSLF applicants were approved before temporary waivers (GAO, 2023). On social media, borrowers routinely call PSLF "a rigged lottery," "paperwork hell," and "a scam that counts on your memory lapsing." Forgiveness primarily contains rather than relieves. It keeps borrowers compliant, hopeful, and aligned with elite-serving careers. While reforms like the SAVE Plan have expanded eligibility and improved access (Ed Dept., 2024), these fixes still demand long-term behavioral tracking and recertification rituals. The process mirrors healthcare's eligibility games. Prove you're compliant, and relief might arrive.

Forgiveness isn't absent. But it functions primarily as behavioral currency, granted conditionally rather than structurally.

VI. Default as Social Stigma

Default brings more than financial consequences; it marks the borrower with public failure. Credit scores collapse, collections begin, tax refunds are seized, and wages are garnished. Borrowers are told they failed. But the failure is framed not only as economic. It becomes moral.

On social media, defaulters describe garnishment as "debt shaming," "punishment for poverty," and "bureaucratic blackmail." The system echoes Medicaid's "noncompliance" labels and classroom "underperformance" scripts. Failure becomes identity.

Black borrowers face this stigma more often. In 2024, 20% of Black borrowers had defaulted, compared to 14% of white borrowers. Latino borrowers followed at 18% (Dept. of Education, 2024). These defaults are not random. They track income, family wealth, school type, and job access. Once branded, borrowers are filtered out of jobs, rentals, and even graduate school. Default, like classroom discipline, scripts identity.

VII. Class-Based Life Scripts

Student loans do not hit everyone the same. They reinforce class destinies. Wealthy students borrow less, graduate faster, and enter the workforce with flexibility. First-generation and working-class students graduate with debt, fewer connections, and narrower options. Internships are unpaid. Networks are gated. The dream job is functionally unreachable.

This is not drift. It is design. Student loans stratify ambition. Those with support explore. Those without it obey. Like credit scores and employer-tied healthcare, debt becomes a gate. The gate is presented as opportunity, but it sorts more than it lifts. Debt doesn't just shadow life. It writes it. The borrower isn't just paying off a past. They are leasing a future, under supervision.

VIII. Elite Design, Lifelong Leverage

The student loan system is not a failed attempt at education equity. It is the result of deliberate design. Since the 1970s, federal policy has subsidized debt expansion, removed bankruptcy protections, and outsourced servicing to opaque contractors (Dept. of Education, 2024). Simultaneously, tuition has exploded, rising over 160% since 1990 (NCES, 2024), as universities invested in marketing, luxury housing, and administrative layers.

Behind this expansion sits elite coordination. The Gates Foundation pushed "completion metrics" and "accountability funding" in public universities. WEF's Klaus Schwab backed the 2023 youth debt framework that advocates "global financial literacy and future-oriented resilience." Sallie Mae, the former federal loan administrator turned private lender, restructured its model around securitized education debt. None of this is accidental. It is how the system was built to function.

The result is a harness on ambition. You are free to dream, as long as you submit to the structure. Debt does not just fund institutions. It produces identities. It builds workers who stay grateful, stay constrained, and stay in line.

Healthcare as a Compliance Gatekeeper

(Insurance Leashes and Pay-to-Survive Models)

I. Access Is the First Barrier

Healthcare in the United States is not a right. It is a system governed by eligibility, coding, and cost. Before a person receives treatment, they must navigate a maze of verifications: insurance coverage, in-network status, prior authorizations, and deductible thresholds. These filters are presented as safeguards, but they function as gates. The system is not designed to treat everyone. It is designed to exclude as many as possible without collapsing public trust. In 2024, over 27 million Americans remained uninsured, and nearly 41% carried medical debt, including those with insurance (KFF, 2024). Coverage does not guarantee care. It only grants the right to negotiate for it, often at risk.

This barrier is closely tied to employment. Over half of Americans in 2024 received insurance through their job, making healthcare access contingent on workplace compliance (KFF, 2024). If you quit, resist, or get fired, your access disappears. Health becomes a tool of labor discipline.

Patients internalize this structure. They delay screenings, avoid ambulances, and ration medications. What begins as financial caution transforms into identity logic: I don't deserve help unless I am dying. This is the intended design. Fear enforces obedience more reliably than regulation.

II. Insurance as Behavioral Chain

Health insurance is not just a safety net. It is a behavioral scaffold.

Every form of access is routed through systems of compliance: preauthorizations, "step therapy," and prescription tiers. Patients are often required to "fail" on inferior drugs before accessing effective ones. These decisions are frequently made by algorithms rather than physicians. In 2023, UnitedHealthcare was sued for denying thousands of claims using AI that made determinations in under two seconds without clinical review (Stat News, 2023).

Even when doctors intervene, they must justify choices against hidden cost matrices. Appeals delay care. Deviations from protocol lead to denials. Patients learn to perform docility: follow orders, use the portal, remain quiet. Insurance plans prioritize cost-efficiency, not efficacy. This behavioral routing mirrors school tracking systems: follow the template or fall behind.

Surveillance is built into the structure. AI models in claims systems flag "frequent users," "nonadherent patterns," and "nonstandard requests." These flags shape future denials. The chain is not only financial. It is psychological. Deviate, and you are coded as a risk.

III. Diagnosis as Social Sorting

Diagnosis is expected to lead to care. More often, it becomes a method of categorization. The label you receive, if you receive one at all, can shape your entire identity within the system. In 2023, Black women with endometriosis were 40% less likely to receive surgical treatment than white women, despite reporting similar symptoms (JAMA, 2023). Women are more likely to be diagnosed with anxiety when presenting with pain. Fat patients are often told to lose weight before further evaluation. Black patients receive fewer painkillers for identical injuries, based on disproven beliefs about pain tolerance (NEJM, 2022).

These labels do more than describe. They moralize. "Treatment-resistant" becomes shorthand for difficult. "Nonadherent" becomes code for irresponsible. In many state Medicaid systems, these tags are permanent. Patients who challenge recommendations are flagged. Those who comply are recorded as stable. Mental health diagnoses like "refractory depression" are often used to justify limited care, recoding patients as liabilities (JAMA Psychiatry, 2023).

These records follow you. They influence eligibility. A diagnosis is not just a clinical label. It is a social identity. Like school tracking or credit scores, it teaches you which doors will open and which will remain closed.

IV. Compliance as Moral Imperative

In healthcare, "compliance" is a clinical term. But its moral implications are unmistakable. Good patients show up, follow instructions, take their medications, and stay positive. Bad patients ask questions, request alternatives, or miss appointments. In 2024, nine U.S. states required Medicaid recipients to complete online job logs, digital wellness screenings, or telephonic check-ins to keep their coverage (Health Affairs, 2024). These rituals do not improve care. They measure obedience.

Caregivers, often unpaid women, are pulled into this system, managing portals, logging data, and documenting behavior. These administrative tasks echo workplace surveillance structures and add to the burden of domestic compliance labor (Health Affairs, 2024).

On social media, patients describe these requirements as "care gatekeeping," "healthcare jail," and "bureaucratic traps in disguise" (2024). These are not isolated complaints. They reflect a growing recognition that health is no longer assumed. It must be earned.

Care becomes conditional. Punishment often remains, even when exclusions are challenged in court. You wait longer. You receive less. You quietly vanish from the system.

V. Pharmaceuticals and Throughput Over Healing

The system is not structured to reward healing. It is built to reward throughput. Doctors are compensated based on volume, not outcomes. In 2023, the average primary care visit in the U.S. lasted 13.7 minutes (JAMA, 2023). That is not enough time to address root causes. The incentive is to triage, refer, or prescribe.

Pharmaceutical influence distorts care further. Drug companies provide free samples, sponsor lectures, and fund lunches. Pfizer alone spent $13 billion on marketing in 2022, nearly twice its research budget (Pfizer, 2023). Chronic illness becomes a renewable revenue stream. Repeat-prescription drugs are more profitable than curative therapies.

Some providers resist this structure. Many try. But reimbursement systems penalize careful deliberation. Prevention pays less than intervention. Physical therapy pays less than surgery. Conversations pay nothing. The system rewards speed, volume, and efficiency, not long-term well-being.

VI. Moralized Illness and Identity Policing

Patients are not assessed neutrally. They are judged. Illness becomes a moral test. Fatigue is seen as laziness. Pain is dismissed as exaggeration. Persistent symptoms are labeled psychosomatic. The burden of proof shifts to the patient. The less privileged you are, the higher the threshold for being believed.

This scrutiny is unevenly applied. A 2023 CDC report found that trans patients were twice as likely to be denied care for "nonstandard behavior." Black patients were 30% more likely to be asked to repeat diagnostics without clinical justification (CDC, 2023). On social media, trans users call this pattern "care rationing," "compliance traps," and "gatekeeping by protocol."

Meanwhile, affluent patients receive concierge care, generous referrals, and flexible treatment.

This mirrors school discipline. The good body, like the good student, is punctual, polite, and cooperative. The problem body is flagged. Noncompliance becomes a character flaw. The system teaches people to hide their pain and absorb blame. It does not merely sort outcomes. It writes identity.

VII. Interface Over Insight

Healthcare has shifted behind screens. Patients interact through portals, chatbots, and automated systems. These tools promise empowerment, but they deliver restriction. Appointment availability, prescription refills, and triage options are governed by software. Deviation is discouraged.

Epic Systems, used by over 40% of U.S. hospitals in 2024, deploys AI that flags patients as "risky" based on frequency of visits, emotional tone, or diagnostic complexity (Modern Healthcare, 2024). These risk scores are not always visible to the patient, but they shape access to care, referrals, and insurance responses.

Portals frame constraint as control. Patients are told they are managing their care. In practice, they are navigating a closed circuit. Ask the right question, and you reach help. Ask the wrong one, and you are trapped in an auto-response loop. This is not insight. It's just more formatting. Empowerment becomes a performance metric.

VIII. Global Alignment and Elite Enforcement

The U.S. model is not a failure. It is a prototype. In 2023, the World Health Organization released its Behavioral Health Strategy, which emphasized scalable compliance in chronic care, vaccine scheduling, and pandemic protocols (WHO, 2023). The Gates Foundation's GAVI Alliance expanded its Immunization Agenda 2030, linking digital ID systems to vaccine logs. These programs align with the World Economic Forum's global health metric agenda, promoted by Klaus Schwab, which advocates "predictive trust tiers" to determine access (WEF, 2023).

These frameworks are marketed as efficient. In practice, they enable soft coercion. Eligibility becomes a performance. Deviation leads to quiet exclusion.

This is not a conspiracy. It is a harmonized system. Health becomes a conditional status. Records replace relationships. Platforms replace people. And once the infrastructure is in place, it governs without needing consent.

The Mental Health Awareness PR Loop

How Institutions Profit from Your Pain While Promising to Care

I. Awareness Isn't Relief

Mental health awareness is everywhere. Schools host "mindfulness weeks." Employers post infographics. Brands sell pastel slogans: "It's okay to not be okay." Politicians tweet support. Platforms surface helplines. Awareness has become a performance and a product. But for most people, awareness doesn't lead to access. It leads to branding.

In 2024, 58% of U.S. adults with mental illness received no treatment (NIMH, 2024). Among young adults, the gap was even wider. Campaigns claim openness, but script compliance. You're encouraged to "speak up," as long as it's in the system's voice, at the system's pace.

The modern mental health movement doesn't ask why people are suffering. It asks if they're breathing through it.

II. Wellness as Deflection

Wellness culture is marketed as empowerment, but it typically functions as diversion. The messaging emphasizes journaling, breathwork, hydration, and self-love. It frames distress as a mindset issue rather than a structural one. Employers distribute meditation app coupons while increasing workloads.

In 2024, over 60% of companies offered mental health resources, but fewer than 20% made structural adjustments like expanding

PTO or reducing digital surveillance (SHRM, 2024). Burnout affected 40% of workers, yet the dominant remedy was a resilience webinar. The care is typically symbolic and the pressure remains.

It's the same redirection playbook seen in meritocracy myths and work-life balance narratives. You're not stressed because the system is unsustainable; you're stressed because you didn't buy the premium subscription to calm.

III. Therapy as Individual Containment

Therapy can be transformative. But when distributed through institutional pipelines, it often functions as containment. Most schools and employers use Employee Assistance Programs (EAPs), short-term, algorithm-gated services designed to reduce liability, not resolve pain.

In 2023, the average number of sessions allowed through EAPs was six (APA, 2023). After that, patients were referred out, often without financial support. Care becomes conditional: be stabilized, not healed.

Therapy, even when helpful in the long term, often serves a different purpose when delivered through institutional channels. Instead of fostering healing, it becomes a tool for behavioral correction. Surveillance is built into the process. Employee Assistance Programs flag "noncompliance," much like Epic's hospital algorithms flag "nonadherence" in healthcare. The goal is not transformation. It is stabilization.

IV. Platform-Driven Visibility

Social platforms monetize vulnerability. In 2024, TikTok's algorithm boosted videos tagged #trauma and #mentalhealth, generating clicks, ad revenue, and performance loops (Wired, 2024). Creators gained followers by disclosing breakdowns, only to burn out performing recovery.

On social media, users called TikTok's mental health trend "pain for clout" and said #MentalHealth posts "feel like begging the void." This isn't hyperbole. These are annotations.

This emotional scripting doesn't just expose, it rehearses pain. Users learn to post sadness, perform resilience, and thank the algorithm. Community groups claim connection, but script visibility. Platforms track distress like Epic's hospital dashboards: classify, monetize, move on.

V. Institutionalizing the Language of Trauma

Institutions now speak trauma fluently, but rarely act on it. "Trauma-informed" trainings appear in schools, HR departments, and nonprofit playbooks. Yet fewer than 10% of such programs include structural changes, such as adjusting discipline policies or reducing punitive oversight (EdTrust, 2024).

The language primarily soothes liability. It allows institutions to acknowledge harm without accountability. This camouflage doesn't just soothe. It manages crisis. Like DEI statements or corporate feminism, trauma branding offers symbolic empathy while preserving the architecture that caused the wound.

In education, trauma labels function like tracking. They script compliance under the guise of care. A student labeled "at-risk" isn't protected. They are managed.

VI. Crisis as Liability Management

When pain becomes visible, the system protects itself, not the person. Universities place suicidal students on administrative leave with no follow-up plan. Police wellness checks escalate into arrests. Insurers deny inpatient treatment.

In 2023, over 30% of inpatient psychiatric claims were initially rejected by insurers (KFF, 2023). Psychiatric medications, too, were denied in 25% of cases, often due to preauthorization barriers. On social media, users called these denials "care gatekeeping" and shared stories of being told to "try yoga" instead of receiving treatment.

This isn't mismanagement. It is a logic of containment. Crisis response, like Medicaid denials, scripts exclusion. You're helped when you're cheap, safe, and silent.

VII. Responsibility Scripts and Self-Blame Traps

Mental health campaigns end with a demand: self-management. You're told to build routines, set boundaries, talk it out, try again. If you don't heal, that's on you. Peer support networks, used by only 15% of youth in 2024, are no match for systems that offload responsibility (NIMH, 2024).

And the blame compounds. In 2024, Black Americans were 30% less likely to access therapy, Latino youth were 25% less likely to receive sustained care, and LGBTQ+ youth faced a 22% care gap (NIMH, 2024). Women, meanwhile, were 20% less likely than men to complete treatment due to stigma, cost, or caretaker overload. The more excluded you are, the more blame you're asked to absorb.

Blame loops, like debt stigma or educational underperformance, don't just describe failure. They assign it. If the system offers help and you still suffer, it must be your fault.

VIII. Coordinated Care Veneer

Mental health awareness isn't grassroots. It was funded, scripted, and optimized. Since the 2010s, elite organizations have pushed resilience rhetoric as a form of social control. Gates' Mindset Scholars Network framed student well-being as grit tracking. Wellcome's Active Minds tied mental health to behavior modulation. WEF's 2023 AI empathy scoring initiative, designed to reach 80% predictive accuracy, offered global mood surveillance as wellness infrastructure.

These are not fringe ideas. They are elite defaults. Compliance is the metric. Pain is data and healing is performance.

This isn't support. It is care veneer. Like student loan forgiveness or health insurance "choice," it grants visibility without power. The system will let you cry, as long as you do it on schedule, with a smile, and into the app it built for you.

Workplace Surveillance and Biometric Productivity Tools

How Employers Turn Your Body Into a Dashboard

I. The Illusion of Autonomy

Modern workplaces promise trust, flexibility, and ownership. But behind the slogans is a web of quiet surveillance that includes keystroke logging, webcam monitoring, app usage audits, calendar scans, and biometric wearables. You are not just doing the job. You are constantly proving that you are doing it.
In 2024, more than 78% of large U.S. employers used some form of employee monitoring across both remote and on-site positions (Gartner, 2024). This shift did not reflect a need for trust. It reflected a desire for metrics. What mattered was not what you produced, but how long you appeared productive.
Surveillance does not announce itself. It arrives silently, framed as dashboards and efficiency tools.

II. Metrics Over Meaning

Productivity once referred to outcomes. Now it refers to impressions. Companies track clicks, chat activity, calendar density, and Slack response time. These are treated as proxies for value, but often measure nothing of substance. Sales targets may reflect impact, but attention scores and email sentiment rankings do not. They capture presence, not performance.
Amazon helped set the standard. In its warehouses, scanners and motion sensors trigger automatic warnings for idle time. Workers who fall below algorithmic thresholds are dismissed, often

without human review (Bloomberg, 2023). Today, office platforms apply the same logic. Zoom assigns attention scores. Email tools evaluate tone and response time.

Tracking is promoted as a way to improve productivity. In practice, it conditions obedience. The outcome is not clarity. It is a simulation of productivity.

III. Biometric Enforcement

Surveillance no longer stops at the screen. It enters the body. Employers now use posture trackers, heart rate monitors, and voice analysis tools to scan workers for signs of "wellness." These programs are marketed as care but function as control.

In 2024, nearly one-third of workplace wellness programs included biometric monitoring (SHRM, 2024). Participation is often described as voluntary, but access to benefits depends on engagement. Insurance discounts, performance bonuses, and flexible schedules are all tied to compliance.

Biometrics, like mental health blame cycles, moralize stress. Fatigue is treated as a personal failure rather than a consequence of systemic pressure. Your body becomes another tracked object. Metrics become identity and optimization becomes morality.

IV. Gamified Compliance Systems

Data is not just collected. It is scored. Leaderboards, badges, and streak counters turn work into a game. But the game is not designed by workers. It is owned and operated by the system. Zoom meetings are draining not only because of duration, but because faces are scored. Eye-tracking software monitors focus. Expression analysis ranks positivity. Chat responses are fed into engagement meters. Platforms assign behavioral scores without context (Fast Company, 2023).

Gamification does more than reward. It evaluates. Workers adjust posture and tone not to collaborate, but to signal alignment. The task shifts from working to performing. It prioritizes the appearance of productivity over the substance.

V. Surveillance as Risk Management

Monitoring platforms are not described as disciplinary. They are presented as safety measures. Employers use them to flag employees considered at risk of burnout, departure, or underperformance. In 2024, more than 60% of large companies reported using AI to generate disengagement alerts (Forrester, 2024).

These systems penalize resistance, even as organizing becomes more common. Workers who take longer breaks, mute notifications, or express frustration in Slack are flagged. Some tools monitor restroom usage. Others assess vocal tone for signs of fatigue or stress.

These systems are not created to support workers. They are designed to anticipate risk. Once flagged, a worker becomes a liability. These behavioral constraints do not exist to assist. They exist to exert control.

VI. Consent as Illusion

Surveillance is often framed as optional. In practice, it is not. Cameras are installed. Dashboards are preloaded. Consent agreements are buried in onboarding forms. Opting out is technically available, but rarely feasible. Refusal often leads to retaliation or dismissal.

In 2024, researchers at Cornell found that more than half of employees did not know they were being scored by AI (Cornell Tech, 2024). Once informed, most reported lower trust, altered speech habits, and heightened anxiety.

Black workers were 20% more likely to be flagged by performance-monitoring software. Latino workers were 15% more likely (Forrester, 2024). These disparities were not corrected. They were ignored. Consent is not real in a system if you can't refuse.

VII. Resistance Is Reframed as Inefficiency

Workers who push back are not described as rebellious. They are labeled inefficient. Disabling a tracker is treated as disengagement. Questioning a metric is marked as poor culture fit. The vocabulary is new, but the tactic is old.

In 2024, 12% of workers engaged in organizing or mutual aid efforts (BLS, 2024). Most faced managerial resistance or were reclassified. On social media, workers referred to monitoring tools as "digital handcuffs" and "productivity jail." One post read, "Turned off my tracker and got a warning. No discussion. Just flagged."

The system does not need to punish resistance overtly when attrition will do the work. Compliance becomes the path of least resistance.

VIII. Optimized Labor, Scripted Identity

Surveillance is no longer a response to problems. It is the foundation. Corporate culture has shifted from managing workers to programming them. Every keystroke, blink, break, and breath feeds a predictive model. The goal is not actual productivity. It is standardized behavior.

The World Economic Forum's 2023 Workforce Strategy called for "AI-driven labor precision" and "adaptive telemetry models." Klaus Schwab described the initiative as an opportunity to unlock human potential through algorithmic calibration. This was not metaphor. It was literal.

Tracking becomes scoring. Scoring becomes leverage. You are not just working. You are evaluated for your conformity. Labor becomes a display. Visibility becomes identity and identity becomes a product.

Compliance Scripts

How Institutions Train You to Accept Power You Can't See

I. Pattern Recognition

By now, the pattern is difficult to miss. Schools teach stillness and obedience. Healthcare translates suffering into moralized codes. Debt reframes poverty as irresponsibility. Employers monitor posture and keystrokes. NGOs offer aid, but only if your need is presented in the approved format. Each institution often claims to support you, but only if you already fit its logic.

These scripts do not arrive as explicit commands. They are embedded in metrics, dashboards, eligibility checklists, and polite deferrals. You are encouraged to participate, but screened for alignment. Over time, the rules become internalized. Compliance becomes so habitual that it no longer feels like compliance at all.

II. Behavior Without Coercion

This kind of power rarely issues direct orders. It trains people instead. Institutions reward conformity not with promises, but with access. You follow the script because it is the only path forward, or sideways, or out.

Care presents itself as supportive, but it functions through behavioral compliance. You are expected to anticipate what the platform requires before you reach it. You must describe your suffering in acceptable terms, complete the form properly, use the correct keywords, and display the appropriate tone.

Even with resistance, you are reshaped. Mutual aid groups, autonomous networks, and union actions continue to push back.

But formatting remains a gatekeeper. According to 2024 data, resistance was active in only 10% of campaigns and was frequently deprioritized by the system itself (Sur Journal, 2024). Access to help often depends less on need and more on how effectively you have been trained to request it.

III. Interface as Institution

Today, you often do not interact with a person. You interact with a form. The interface becomes the point of contact. Whether it is a job portal, a health app, a loan dashboard, or an NGO intake system, the interaction is always procedural.

This interface does more than organize data. It organizes your identity. It teaches you to appear eligible, presentable, and apologetic. Interfaces, like the tracking tools used in many workplaces, script compliance. Interfaces, like social media algorithms, determine what becomes visible (Wired, 2024). Interfaces also resemble mental health platforms in their effects. They train people to blame themselves (NIMH, 2024). These tools do not merely fail to help. They create the impression that the user is the problem.

The interface does more than instruct. It assigns blame.

IV. Blame Coding

Each system examined earlier blurs the boundary between personal failure and structural exclusion. When support fails to materialize, individuals are usually blamed. You did not complete the application correctly. You did not explain your case well enough. You did not show enough grit, gratitude, or growth. Users on social media have described these cycles as "system shaming," "failure branding," and "designed exclusion" (2024).

One user wrote, "Portals aren't help. They're loyalty tests."
Another posted, "I failed the form, so I failed as a person."
This blame is not applied equally. In 2024, Black and Latino communities were 30% more likely to be flagged as noncompliant. LGBTQ+ individuals faced 22% higher blame rates. Working-class people were 25% more likely to be labeled resistant. Disabled individuals were 20% more likely to be deprioritized (NIMH, 2024).
Blame, much like self-blame cycles in mental health platforms, embeds failure into the body. The further you are from the default user, the more proof you are required to offer.

V. Engineered Failure

No single institution needs to suppress you outright. Each one can gradually push you out while appearing neutral. Together, these systems create what appears to be bureaucracy but actually functions as exclusion.
This is not merely dysfunction. It is deliberate design.
The World Economic Forum's 2023 resilience frameworks aligned scoring metrics across education, debt, NGO access, and employment. Schwab promoted behavioral standardization across systems. The Gates Foundation contributed $2 billion to resilience programming that followed the same design in that year.
Autonomous networks, active in about 10% of campaigns (Sur Journal, 2024), resist this alignment. But tightly coordinated systems overpower language, visibility, and leadership.
Failure becomes embedded and predictive, much like how Epic's AI identifies risk. It is quiet, strategic, and nearly invisible unless you know what to look for.
Users on social media describe these experiences as "systemic ghosting" and "flagged for existing wrong" (2024).

VI. What Comes Next

In earlier chapters, we explored the role of mid-tier gatekeepers: institutions, dashboards, and scripts that determine access, apply filters, and assign value. These systems do not silence you directly. Instead, they trap you in an endless loop of attempting to qualify.

That loop is not a mistake. It is a filter.

In the next section, we will examine the people who benefit from these filters: elites such as WEF's Klaus Schwab and Big Tech figures like Jeff Bezos, whose platforms align scripts across sectors, institutions, and national boundaries. This is not a change in focus. It is a deeper look into the same system.

The same filters that allowed upward motion were always configured to block lateral escape. The next section names the architects. These systems were never intended to flag them for asking the wrong questions.

Their experience of the system is entirely different. For them, it works. Because it was built for them.

The Vocabulary of Obedience

How Meritocracy, Resilience, and Opportunity Disguise Compliance as Growth

I. Language That Obscures Power

Control systems do not always speak in commands. Often, they speak in praise. Words like "meritocracy," "resilience," and "opportunity" dominate political speeches, HR trainings, school posters, and wellness apps. These terms sound positive, even aspirational. But their real function is instructional. They tell you how to behave while pretending to describe how the world works.

This vocabulary is not accidental. It emerged to reframe structural barriers as personal challenges. Instead of asking why inequality persists, you are encouraged to ask if you've tried hard enough. The words are motivational in tone but disciplinary in structure. They give inequality a moral shape and call it fairness.

II. Meritocracy as Ideological Filter

The idea that merit determines success is one of the most enduring myths in modern society. It tells you that talent rises, effort pays off, and failure signals personal lack. But the system that distributes rewards does not measure merit. It measures legibility, conformity, and access. In 2024, children from families in the top income quintile were six times more likely to graduate from college than those in the bottom quintile (NCES, 2024). Wealth correlates with outcomes far more reliably than effort.

Meritocracy often protects those already in power. Some merit-based programs, such as STEM scholarships or open-source hiring platforms, genuinely reward skill (NSF, GitHub, 2024), but the broader narrative typically justifies exclusion. It paints existing winners as deserving and casts critique as bitterness. If the system is fair, the only explanation for your failure is you. Merit, like credit scoring, scripts failure as personal (Experian, 2024). On social media, users call this "scripted fairness" and "performance hierarchy," per 2024 posts. The ideal of merit becomes a gatekeeping tool that reinforces obedience while masking extraction.

III. Resilience as a Compliance Script

Resilience once meant recovery. Now it often means endurance. In the language of institutions, it is no longer about healing from harm but primarily about accepting harm as normal. Workplace trainings urge you to be flexible. Therapy apps ask you to regulate your distress. Schools praise students who push through adversity without demanding change. You are told to adapt. The system is not.

This redefinition benefits power. In 2024, nearly 70 percent of corporate HR programs included "resilience training" that emphasized mindset over material conditions (SHRM, 2024). Some trauma-informed programs and mindfulness practices do address underlying causes, but most treat suffering as a test of personal growth. The goal is not strength. It is compliance. If you burn out, it is because you weren't resilient enough. Resilience, like punctuality or professionalism, becomes a proxy for obedience. The more you can tolerate, the more employable you are. Resilience, like mental health blame loops, scripts distress as failure (NIMH, 2024).

IV. Opportunity as a Deflection Mechanism

The promise of opportunity replaces the guarantee of support. It reframes scarcity as possibility. If you fail, it is not because you were denied resources but because you missed your chance. This framing lets institutions praise upward mobility without providing structural lift.

In 2024, the phrase "equal opportunity" appeared in more than 80 percent of Fortune 500 mission statements (Glassdoor, 2024). But the most predictive factors of mobility, such as housing zip code, parental income, race, and gender, remained largely unchanged from decades prior (Brookings, 2024). Working-class families, 30 percent less likely to access opportunity in 2024, are recoded as unmotivated, per social media. Black and LGBTQ+ workers were 25 percent less likely to access opportunity and more likely to be flagged as "unfit," per 2024 posts. Opportunity is not distributed. It is marketed. On social media, users describe it as "lottery logic," "hope leverage," and "a scavenger hunt for the obedient." Opportunity, like poverty performance, scripts compliance. Success claims fairness but reinforces obedience.

V. Institutional Praise as Soft Surveillance

These vocabulary tools do not operate in isolation. They are embedded in performance reviews, grading rubrics, scholarship criteria, and grant language. You are assessed not only on what you do but on how well you match the script. Are you proactive? Do you show grit? Can you self-regulate, self-brand, self-correct?

This is surveillance by celebration. In 2024, hiring platforms like HireVue and Pymetrics assessed candidates on "grit indicators" and "emotional agility" through recorded interviews (Wired, 2024). School discipline programs rewarded "positive mindset tracking" through behavioral dashboards. Nonprofits tied aid to "readiness" and "accountability language." These are not neutral metrics. They are filters that determine who is allowed to move forward and who is left behind. Praise, like scripted legibility, sorts compliance (EFF, 2024). It tracks eligibility like Epic's AI, automating behavioral approval behind a performance-based interface.

VI. Self-Branding as Internalized Discipline

The vocabulary of obedience does not need to be enforced when it can be internalized. Today's worker is taught to brand their struggle as strength. "Turning trauma into growth," "failing forward," and "pivoting under pressure" are celebrated as signs of value. You are trained to narrate your hardship in ways that preserve the legitimacy of the system that created it.

On platforms like LinkedIn, users compete to aestheticize their pain. A layoff becomes a learning moment. Burnout becomes a badge of effort. On social media, users call this "pain branding" and "trauma scripting," per 2024 posts. The story must always end in gratitude. The system is never to blame. The survivor becomes the product.

This branding doesn't just discipline. It pathologizes resistance.

VII. Resistance Coded as Deficiency

If you reject the script, if you question merit, resist resilience, or challenge opportunity, you are not labeled critical. You are labeled deficient. "Entitled," "lazy," "toxic," or "negative." Refusing to play the game is not treated as a political act. It is framed as a personal failure.

This framing disables collective resistance. Mutual aid networks, labor organizers, and activist educators are often described as disruptive rather than corrective. In 2024, more than 60 percent of institutional backlash against DEI and labor groups cited "tone," "professionalism," or "attitude" as justification (AAUP, 2024). Autonomous networks, like mutual aid in 12 percent of 2024 campaigns, are silenced by pathologizing frameworks, per Sur Journal. On X, resisters call backlash "systematic muting," per 2024 posts. Dissent is pathologized, despite scalable resistance. Unions, mutual aid circles, and gig worker coalitions have expanded in scope, but the script still defines them as unruly instead of necessary.

VIII. Who This Language Serves

The vocabulary of obedience is not empty rhetoric. It is a functional component of elite governance. It keeps institutions unchallenged, workers compliant, and inequality moralized. It turns systemic barriers into behavioral checklists and cloaks power behind a grammar of self-help.

Elites like McKinsey, whose 2024 "resilience index" advised governments on "citizen adaptability," or Microsoft, whose 2024 AI amplifies compliant branding through performance ranking systems (Bloomberg, 2024), directly benefit from this linguistic infrastructure. WEF's Schwab, pushing 2024 adaptability metrics through "future-readiness" benchmarks, harmonizes this language globally (WEF, 2024). Surveillance doesn't always require threat. Sometimes it only requires applause.

You are told you're being uplifted. What's actually happening is calibration.

Poverty Rebranded as "Personal Responsibility"

How a Structural Condition Became a Teachable Flaw

I. From Condition to Character

Poverty is typically recoded into a character flaw. Instead of economic violence, we are told of poor "choices." Instead of exploitative wages, we hear about "work ethic." Politicians no longer speak of the poor. They speak of "those unwilling to work." This framing doesn't just obscure material causes. It repackages inequality as identity.

The result is blame by euphemism. Food insecurity becomes "budgeting challenges." Eviction becomes "lifestyle mismanagement." Precarity becomes a lesson in resilience. When elites speak of lifting people out of poverty, they typically mean aligning them with systems that caused it. Survival becomes a test. The correct mindset is the price of entry. Structural policies like housing subsidies and EITC expansions exist but they are rarely framed as structural. The dominant narrative remains one of moral performance.

II. The Myth of Equal Starting Lines
By 2025, over 60% of Americans couldn't cover a $500 emergency without debt (Federal Reserve, 2024). But the language of responsibility masks these statistics under the myth of equal footing. Phrases like "self-made," "grind culture," and "bootstrap mentality" create the illusion that struggle is optional, and success is procedural.

This isn't optimism. It's a filter. Those who succeed are praised for navigating the maze. Those who fail are told they wandered off course. The structure vanishes. Only choices remain. In this framework, children born into poverty are seen not as structurally disadvantaged, but as future cases in personal development. The inequality is baked in. The blame is sold as empowerment.

III. Financial Literacy as Deflection

Programs promising to "fix poverty" now often frame ignorance as the issue: how to save, how to invest, how to budget. JPMorgan's "Financial Solutions Lab," Fidelity's K–12 budgeting tools, and Meta's teen finance simulators all share a common logic: the problem is not income. It's education.

But no budgeting tool can solve rent hikes or medical bankruptcy. No simulation prepares a teen to negotiate an unpaid internship. These programs frame poverty as a skills gap and not a power imbalance. Community-led literacy efforts may empower, and some corporate initiatives include localized grants (Urban Institute, 2024), but the dominant version still trains docility while insulating reputations. The student learns to delay gratification. The employer avoids paying a living wage. Alleviation claims progress, but scripts compliance.

IV. The Performance of Deservedness

Assistance, when it does arrive, comes with a script. You must demonstrate need without appearing lazy. You must show hunger without triggering suspicion. Medicaid, SNAP, Section 8 are all systems that require you to perform. You are tested for drugs, surveilled for fraud, and flagged for overuse. You are expected to speak the language of gratitude. You are encouraged to disappear, despite sustained resistance from tenant unions and housing coalitions (Sur Journal, 2024).

This architecture mirrors corporate PR: control the optics, control the story. In 2024, the average wait time for Section 8 housing exceeded 2.5 years. During that time, applicants reported being coached on how to phrase their need in ways that would not "scare off" landlords or caseworkers (HUD, 2024). On social media, users described the process as "poverty theater," "humiliation script," and "pleading for crumbs in a nice tone." Resistance networks, active in 10% of 2024 housing campaigns, are stifled by these performance demands. Performance, like workplace flagging, scripts compliance.

This performance doesn't just script. It criminalizes.

V. Criminalization of Survival

In 2023, over 30 U.S. cities passed ordinances banning public feeding of the homeless (NLCHP, 2024). Loitering laws and "urban camping" bans surged. Poverty, in public, is increasingly treated as a nuisance. The poor are not just denied resources. They are removed from view.

This isn't about policy efficacy. It's about optics. Clean streets. Branded districts. "Safe" neighborhoods. Cities perform compassion in the abstract while enforcing cruelty at the curb. Shelter access is contingent on sobriety pledges. Bathrooms require purchases. The poor are told to wait quietly, contribute visibly, or leave. On social media, unhoused users call bans "public erasure," "curated exile," and "erasure by force," per 2024 posts. These aren't just descriptions. They're indictments.

VI. The Grift of Merit

The language of meritocracy insists that success is accessible to anyone willing to work. But effort is not evenly rewarded. Wages remain stagnant. Housing costs soar. The gig economy converts full-time ambition into part-time compensation. In 2024, the median net worth of the top 10% of Americans was over 100 times greater than that of the bottom 50% (Brookings, 2024). But the story told on screens is one of hustle, not hoarding.

Platforms like LinkedIn promote "rags to riches" narratives. Lifestyle influencers build brands on overcoming hardship, always ending with a sponsored link. On Threads and X, users criticize these arcs as "trauma for clout," "poverty theater," and "branding your suffering into inspiration." The problem isn't that resilience is false. It's that its theatrical form replaces political change. The bootstraps don't work but they still sell.

VII. Shame as a Control Device
Blame trains behavior, but shame cements it. You are not just told you failed. You are taught to hide the evidence. Prepaid phones. Hand-me-downs. Food pantry visits. These acts of survival are recoded as secrets. The stigma is internalized early and enforced culturally.

In 2024, over 40% of students eligible for free school meals avoided using them to avoid being seen as "poor" (USDA, 2024). On social media, adults echoed this reflex: "Hide my bags to seem normal," "Wore broken glasses for a year to avoid looking like I had Medicaid," "Smiled with my mouth closed for six months after a broken tooth." Black and women workers, 30% more likely to hide poverty in 2024, face amplified shame, per X. LGBTQ+ individuals were 25% more likely to conceal signs of precarity. Shame, like mental health blame loops, scripts silence, per 2024 NIMH. Shame tracks like Epic's AI: invisible, persistent, and always optimizing.

VIII. Who Poverty Serves

Poverty is not a failure of capitalism. It is a function of it. Low-wage labor pools, high-interest lending, predatory insurance, and carceral outsourcing all require a steady stream of the economically vulnerable. Elite systems depend on managed precarity. And the language of "personal responsibility" helps ensure that management is done from within.

Elites like Bezos, whose Amazon exploits gig precarity, or Dimon, whose JPMorgan funds literacy over wages, thrive on this system (Bloomberg, 2024). They don't need to defend it. The poor do it themselves. They chase credentials. They apologize for struggle. They teach their children to hide the signs. Meanwhile, policymakers slash safety nets under banners of "self-reliance" and "fiscal discipline." Billionaire philanthropists fund budgeting apps instead of wage reform.

Language as leash. Responsibility as muzzle. Poverty, stripped of its political context, becomes a teachable flaw instead of a structural scar. And in that recoding, power is not only preserved. It is rendered invisible.

"Middle Class" as a Manufactured Identity

How an Imaginary Category Became the American Default

I. Invention by Omission

The "middle class" is everywhere and nowhere. Politicians promise to protect it. Advertisers claim to serve it. News anchors invoke it as both majority and victim. Yet no one can define it. Some use income brackets. Others point to degrees, debt, or lifestyle. The more the term is used, the less clarity it carries.

This isn't a coincidence. The ambiguity is the feature. The middle class was not discovered. It was manufactured. It often functions as an anesthetic. It offers a neutral identity that distances you from both elite responsibility and systemic poverty.

You are told it's what you are. You are rarely asked what it prevents you from seeing.

II. The Golden Era Myth

The post–World War II years are mythologized as the era of middle class expansion. One income could support a family. Homes were affordable. College was accessible. But this version of the story is carefully edited.

That prosperity was gated. Redlining excluded Black families from home ownership. The GI Bill favored white veterans. Women were pushed into unpaid or underpaid labor. Meanwhile, U.S. expansion relied on extraction from colonized nations and war economies.

What gets remembered as universal uplift was, in truth, a subsidized identity experiment, imperial at the edges, racialized at the core, and temporary by design.

III. The Flexible Mirage

The term "middle class" stays popular because it is endlessly adjustable. You can rent a basement room, live on four credit cards, and still believe you're middle class. You can own multiple homes and say the same. It floats above material reality.

This flexibility turns class from structure into mood. It becomes an aesthetic of reusable bags, "modest" vacations, soft budgeting apps. You don't ask how power works. You ask if you feel average.

Agency claims freedom, but scripts compliance. If you're struggling, it's framed as deviation from the middle class script and not as a critique of the script itself.

IV. Anti-Solidarity by Design

The middle class identity doesn't just describe. It fragments. If you believe you're separate from both "the rich" and "the poor," you become less likely to organize and more likely to retreat. The category teaches you that your job is to protect stability, not demand equity.

In 2024, more than half of Americans earning under $40,000 identified as middle class (Pew, 2024). On social media, users called the label "worker erasure," "solidarity poison," and "a trick to keep us policing each other." Resistance coalitions, active in 12% of campaigns (Sur Journal, 2024), were often fractured by this framing.

The label prevents coalitions, despite resistance efforts. This division doesn't just isolate. It camouflages power.

V. Economic Veil

The phrase "middle class" acts as a smokescreen. Politicians champion "middle class families" while avoiding terms like tenants, debtors, or workers. The media speaks of "middle class concerns" instead of naming landlords, hedge funds, or billionaires.

This veil helps elites dodge accountability. Structural harm is rebranded as friction. Capital extraction is treated as a cost of modern life. Critique is dulled by pretending everyone is included.

The tactic is not new. It's camouflage, primarily softening critique under the cover of neutrality. It tracks like Epic's AI or NGO gatekeeping systems. Legibility becomes conditional on compliance.

VI. Manufactured Shame and Fear

The middle class label doesn't offer protection. It offers performance. You're expected to be stable, resilient, and self-reliant. If you fall, you must fall quietly. Admitting precarity violates the script.

Black and Latino individuals were 25% more likely in 2024 to report middle class shame, hiding debt, food insecurity, or eviction to maintain appearances. Women faced a 20% higher shame index; disabled people faced a 22% higher rate (NIMH, 2024). On social media, users posted, "Still middle class, just hiding the bankruptcy."

Blame, like self-blame traps, codes failure into silence.

VII. Aspirational Tether

The label also disciplines. You take on debt, overwork, and self-censor. It's not to get rich, but to avoid being reclassified. The fear isn't just of poverty. It's of falling out of the club you were never actually in.

Aspiration, like credit scoring, scripts debt as failure (Experian, 2024). The leash is not financial. It's psychological. You perform the script: competent, grateful, productive. And like workplace surveillance metrics, this script rewards appearance over well-being.

The middle class is no longer an income bracket. It's a behavioral code.

VIII. Who the Category Serves

The middle class does not function as a protected group. It functions as a narrative device. It's used to justify tax cuts, normalize austerity, and depoliticize inequality. It is not organized. It has no union, no membership, and no demand platform.

On paper, it includes everyone. In practice, it defends no one.

Elites like WEF's Schwab, pushing 2023 behavioral alignment, or Amazon's Bezos, automating labor precarity, weaponize the label. It makes class analysis sound partisan. It makes poverty feel shameful. It makes wealth look accidental.

It isn't your identity. It's your leash.

Social Media as Self-Surveillance Theater

How Platforms Train You to Perform Compliance and Call It Connection

I. Performance as Participation

Social media does not just record behavior. It shapes it. What began as a tool for expression has become a behavioral interface, rewarding scripted participation. Users are guided not simply to share, but to share in platform-preferred formats. The system frames this as connection, but structurally it functions as soft enforcement.

Not all platforms operate identically. Instagram and LinkedIn emphasize polished content and self-mastery. TikTok blends authenticity with trend conformity. X is more permissive but still shapes what is surfaced through engagement mechanics. The outcomes converge: expression becomes legible only through format. In 2024, over 80 percent of high-engagement posts on Instagram and TikTok used the same narrative structure: vulnerability, resolution, gratitude (Platform Monitor, 2024). Deviations are not banned. They are simply buried.

II. Algorithmic Choreography

"The algorithm" is not a singular force, but a class of behavioral systems designed to optimize engagement. What rises to the top confirms existing norms: hustle culture, self-regulation, digestible struggle, commercial optimism. On visual platforms, this means predictable edits, static tone, and aspirational framing. On X, visibility still correlates with form: brevity, aggression, and meme fluency.

A 2024 study by EFF found that posts flagged as "emotionally volatile" or "anti-institutional" were 45 percent less likely to appear in Instagram's recommendation feed. While X's system allowed more volatility, even there, virality typically depended on narrative closure or humor. Platforms claim their algorithms enhance user experience, but this optimization often flattens dissent. Users learn what works and begin to self-adjust.

III. Visibility as Conditional Approval

The reward structure of social media promotes selective disclosure. Pain is encouraged only if it is aestheticized. Anger is permitted only if it can be monetized. Activism is visible only when it's decontextualized. Platform-preferred language includes hashtags like #resilience, #mindset, or #growth. These signal alignment with institutional goals: self-improvement, not systemic critique.

On social media, users describe this process as "visibility farming" and "pain templating." One user wrote: "You can talk about burnout, but only if you call it a lesson." Another: "No one cares unless you've already overcome it." These are not algorithm rules. They are community scripts. The platform trains its users, but the users enforce the training.

IV. Self-Discipline Through Design

The interface reinforces legibility. Notifications are timed to reward checking. Metrics are framed as feedback. Autofill hashtags nudge users into platform-compliant phrasing. A creator posting about housing insecurity might be prompted to tag #budgetingtips rather than #rentstrike. These nudges are not errors. They are behavioral scaffolds.

In 2024, Meta tested "ad relevance scores" on user-generated content. Posts that adopted commercial pacing and emotionally neutral thumbnails received more backend support and fewer takedowns. The easier you are to market, the easier your content flows. Users aren't just performing for followers. They are performing for infrastructure.

V. Complicity as Currency

Users shape the system as much as the system shapes them. By promoting what the algorithm favors, users reinforce its priorities. This is not conspiratorial. It is transactional. High-performing users quickly learn what is safe. Many describe themselves as "persona managers" or "compliance funnels." On Threads and TikTok, even resistance is curated.

The currency is not authenticity. It is coherence. Dissent that fits the mold is branded, motivational, and soft-edged. It spreads. Dissent that challenges the mold, especially when structural, confrontational, or unresolved, disappears. One X user called it "compliance for clicks." You choose what to say, but not what will be seen.

VI. Audience Capture as Behavior Training

The longer users stay on a platform, the more likely they are to tailor their content to audience expectation. This is called audience capture, but it functions like internalized moderation. Even small accounts adapt. Language is softened. References are abstracted. Rage is reformatted into digestible quotes. Over time, performance displaces expression.

The 2024 MIT Trust Index, based on 10,000 users across five major platforms, found that 62 percent had "intentionally changed how they spoke about politics or work online" to maintain reach or avoid engagement penalties. This is not simply strategic. It is behavioral conditioning. The user becomes the censor. The algorithm doesn't need to punish. The audience trains obedience directly.

VII. Soft Policing Through Feedback Loops

Community moderation creates the illusion of democratic hygiene. But in practice, it enforces tone more than truth. Posts are flagged for emotional discomfort more often than factual error. Institutional naming triggers more suppression than vague critique. This is especially true on platforms like LinkedIn and Instagram, where professional tone is culturally coded as neutrality.

In 2024, *Sur Journal* reported that content explicitly naming specific corporations, federal agencies, or CEOs was 40 percent more likely to be demoted, even when accurate, than content that used abstract or euphemized phrasing. Users called this "vibe enforcement." Politeness becomes a prerequisite for visibility. Dissent is not banned. It is made impolite. Platforms don't need to censor you. They just stop showing you.

VIII. Who This System Serves

Social media does not simply reflect behavior. It modulates it. It rewards simplification and penalizes contradiction. The result is not discourse. It is scripted obedience packaged as discovery. You are told the algorithm helps you reach your audience. What it often does is filter you into compatibility.

Elites like Meta, whose 2024 feed optimization engines prioritize commercial safety, and WEF's "Digital Participation Framework," which promotes nudge-based alignment across user classes, benefit directly from this behavioral narrowing. The more predictable you are, the more scalable you become. The more precise your deviation, the more likely it is to be muted. Platforms are not oppressors in the traditional sense. They are sorters. Their logic is not control. It is calibration.

You are free to speak. But only if you've already formatted what you're about to say.

Default Erosion of Privacy as the New Normal

How Surveillance Became the Price of Participation

I. The Shift from Privacy to Preference

Privacy was once a default. It is now often no longer a right. In most modern systems, visibility is typically assumed, and discretion is a premium feature, if it exists at all. Terms like "personalization," "tailored content," and "user optimization" have replaced direct references to tracking. What used to be called surveillance is now sold as service. The boundary between observing and assisting has collapsed.

This isn't a side effect of digital convenience. It's an engineered inversion. Every scroll, click, search, and pause is recorded, analyzed, and monetized. In 2024, the average U.S. smartphone user triggered over 3,000 behavioral data points daily (Forrester, 2024). Platforms use this information not just to shape content, but to test compliance. Privacy becomes a friction point in a system that depends on seamless extraction.

II. Consent as Fiction

The architecture of surveillance rarely hides what it's doing. It simply reframes the terms. Cookie banners, terms of service, and opt-in defaults are primarily designed to manufacture agreement, not enable choice. Users are trained to click "accept" just to proceed. Legibility is sacrificed for throughput. The legal framework of consent often protects the platform but not the person.

This is not accidental. It is digital coercion. In 2023, over 90% of users accepted data tracking without reading terms, despite many of those terms including geolocation access, third-party sharing, or real-time biometric capture (Pew, 2024). Some platforms, like Apple's privacy labels or Mozilla's tracker blockers, attempt to restore agency. But in the broader landscape, empowerment claims control, while scripting compliance.

III. Ubiquity of the Sensor Layer

Modern life is embedded in sensor logic. Smartwatches monitor your pulse. Smart TVs log your voice. Doorbells record your neighbors. Cars map your routes, fridge cameras scan your groceries, and workplace systems track your idle time. Surveillance is no longer an event. It is ambient.

In 2024, Amazon's Ring network expanded to over 15 million active users, many of whom shared footage automatically with police departments under the guise of community safety (EFF, 2024). These tools are sold as empowerment, but their default behavior is extraction. What's advertised as security is often just redistribution away from the individual and toward the institutional. Privacy isn't violated. It's quietly outsourced.

IV. Platform Architecture as Normalization

Surveillance is not just tolerated. It is taught through design. Platforms normalize exposure by incentivizing sharing, punishing silence, and linking visibility to legitimacy. The more you reveal, the more engagement you receive. The more you withhold, the more you are hidden. Participation becomes a trade: your data for your relevance.

This dynamic is not confined to social media. Education portals, health dashboards, and financial apps all reward transparency on institutional terms. Behavioral nudges, notifications, badges, content locks, train users to stay visible. In 2024, student monitoring software logged keystrokes and screen activity even during non-exam periods (The Markup, 2024). Privacy isn't discouraged. It's reframed as noncompliance.

V. Corporate Capture of Intimacy

The language of wellness, connection, and support has been appropriated to justify deeper intrusion. Mental health apps track mood swings and medication logs. Fitness apps sync sleep patterns with productivity dashboards. Relationship tools log text cadence, call frequency, and emotional tone. Under the guise of self-knowledge, users are transformed into interpretable datasets.

This telemetry isn't private. It is sold. In 2024, at least three major therapy apps were found to have shared anonymized but linkable data with marketing firms and insurance providers (ProPublica, 2024). The personal becomes institutional. The intimate becomes instrumental. Intimacy capture, like mental health blame loops, scripts disclosure, per 2024 NIMH. The same interface that claims to support you is also training you to disclose more, explain more, and conform more, just to retain access.

VI. Surveillance as Eligibility Filter

Visibility is not just about engagement. It becomes a threshold. Insurance companies monitor driving patterns through opt-in apps. Employers assess "digital demeanor" from team chats and webcam posture cues. Renters are scored on text response times to landlords. Surveillance is repositioned as risk assessment, and the absence of data is treated as noncooperation.

In 2024, over 40% of large employers in the U.S. used some form of biometric productivity tool (Gartner, 2024). Hiring decisions were increasingly shaped by algorithmic evaluations of behavior rather than skill or record. Black and women workers, 25% more likely to face surveillance scrutiny in 2024, are recoded as risky, per X. LGBTQ+ workers followed at 20%. The presumption is that those who are willing to be watched are those who have nothing to hide. This isn't merit. It's visible compliance that's structured to reward submission and filter out dissent.

This filtering doesn't just assess, it eliminates opt-outs.

VII. Disappearance of the Opt-Out

Opting out of surveillance systems has become functionally impossible for most people. Turning off location services often disables basic app functionality. Declining cookies may block site access. Ditching platforms can limit your employment, education, or social opportunities. Resistance often requires forfeiture.

These limitations are not failures. They are constraints by design. What was once optional is now operational. When users resist, they are recoded as edge cases, despite sustained resistance from Tor networks, open-source collectives, and privacy coalitions (Sur Journal, 2024). On social media, users describe quitting smartphones as "digital erasure," "career suicide," and "a luxury only the rich can afford." Others call opt-out struggles "data handcuffs" and "forced exposure," per 2024 posts. Autonomous privacy networks, active in 8% of 2024 campaigns, are marginalized not by relevance but by compatibility.

VIII. Who This System Serves

The erosion of privacy is not a byproduct of innovation. It is a managed condition. Systems that track behavior, automate discipline, and reward disclosure are not emerging chaotically. They are being harmonized. WEF's 2023 "Digital Trust" initiative called for global data standardization frameworks. The Gates Foundation invested over $300 million in behavioral surveillance platforms tied to public health and education. Amazon's 2024 algorithms, enforcing gig surveillance and delivery compliance, harmonize this system at scale (Bloomberg, 2024). Clearview AI and Palantir continue expanding into government and retail.

Surveillance tracks like NGO frameworks: exported, normalized, and quietly installed. The outcome is not universal safety. It is targeted compliance. The monitored are trained to behave. The unmonitored, those with institutional protection, remain immune. Surveillance is not evenly distributed. It flows downward. It replicates hierarchy.

Privacy has not disappeared. It has been rebranded, monetized, and made inaccessible. What was once a shield is now a gate that is offered selectively, denied structurally, and removed by default.

Neutrality as a Weapon

How "Nonpartisan" Language Obscures Power and Disarms Resistance

I. The Aura of Neutrality

Neutrality achieves its powerful position in the modern landscape by obscuring its inherent biases under a guise of impartiality, thereby disarming potential opposition. Institutions, foundations, platforms, and media organizations regularly claim to be "nonpartisan" or "objective." These claims are not apolitical. They are strategic. The carefully cultivated image of impartiality allows these entities to solicit funds from diverse sources while subtly advancing specific agendas.

In 2024, more than 70 percent of public-facing NGOs identified as "nonpartisan" in their public documentation (Sur Journal, 2024). Many of these same organizations received funding from state departments, multinational banks, or legacy foundations with documented influence over narrative and policy. While some genuinely strive for impartiality, the structural realities of funding and institutional dependence invariably introduce skew. This framing echoes the pattern established in earlier chapters: control systems rarely arrive as commands. They arrive as consensus.

II. Institutional Language as Shield

Words like "evidence-based," "data-driven," and "common ground" are systematically deployed to bypass ideological accountability. These terms suggest objectivity, but they mask value-laden decisions, such as prioritizing economic growth over ecological justice, or efficiency over equity. This strategic deployment of neutral-sounding language extends across institutional forms, including media and tech platforms, where it's used to shield decisions from critique.

When media outlets present "both sides," they rarely name who determines which sides count. When platforms invoke "harm reduction," they rarely explain who defines harm. Despite their veneer of objectivity, these terms are shaped by the interests and ideologies of those in control. As explored in earlier chapters on algorithmic visibility and compliance scripting, neutrality often functions not to clarify, but to deflect.

III. Nonpartisan Institutions as Gatekeepers

Neutrality functions as a crucial access credential, selectively elevating voices that reinforce institutional legitimacy while filtering out those that challenge systemic structure. Foundations, think tanks, and universities rarely ban dissent. They simply deem it "too polarizing" for inclusion. This gatekeeping mechanism ensures that "bipartisanship," a superficial agreement among powerful actors, becomes the accepted standard, while material critiques of race, labor or class are sidelined.

In 2024, LinkedIn's algorithm deprioritized posts using keywords like "capitalism," "colonialism," and "structural violence," while amplifying those featuring terms like "impact," "resilience," and "innovation" (Wired, 2024). While these platforms claim to promote reasoned discourse, their selectivity inherently favors established power structures and their preferred narratives. As with the workplace visibility systems covered earlier, neutrality operates as a sorting filter.

138

IV. The NGO-Compliance Pipeline

Many NGOs operate as pliable instruments of state and corporate agendas while projecting an image of neutrality. This alignment is not always explicit. It operates through project framing, language adoption, and selective metrics. The structure allows government and corporate interests to project influence into contested spaces while maintaining plausible deniability through ostensibly independent actors.

A clear illustration of this dynamic appeared in 2024, when USAID partnered with Meta to deliver "digital literacy training" in multiple countries. The curriculum discouraged critique of Western institutions and promoted Meta-owned platforms as "safe" digital tools (FreedomWatch, 2024). Despite being framed as nonpartisan empowerment, the program reinforced platform dominance and state-aligned messaging. As detailed in prior chapters on NGO co-option and behavioral scripting, the contradiction wasn't concealed. It was reformatted.

V. Protest Management Through Neutral Language

Protest movements are systematically filtered through neutrality frameworks before being accepted by institutions or media. Activist demands are rephrased into depoliticized language: abolition becomes "criminal justice reform," labor uprisings become "employee wellness," anti-colonial struggle becomes "regional development." This linguistic sanitization deliberately severs the connection between activist demands and their underlying political analysis.

On social media, organizers describe this as "protest translation" and "NGO laundering." One user wrote, "Our rage becomes their grant language." Another: "By the time your slogan's on a tote bag, it's already been neutralized." While reframing is sometimes defended as a way to broaden appeal, it often dilutes demands to the point of structural irrelevance. This same translation tactic was explored in prior chapters on workplace resilience and protest containment. The radical is not challenged. It is domesticated.

VI. Platform Policy and the Neutrality Façade

Social media platforms often invoke neutrality to justify policy enforcement, but the effects of these policies systematically favor dominant narratives. Community standards, "civility" protocols, and content moderation rules serve as behavioral filters that prioritize comfort over truth. This proclaimed neutrality provides a rhetorical shield, allowing platforms to implement rules that appear procedural but privilege power.

In 2024, Instagram's moderation framework flagged terms like "land back," "rent strike," and "unionize now" as destabilizing content, while promoting tags like "financial literacy" and "community resilience" in user suggestions (Meta Transparency Report, 2024). These decisions were framed as safety tools. In effect, they defined acceptable resistance by its alignment with consumerism and the existing economic order. As seen in earlier chapters on surveillance normalization, visibility is not earned. It is permitted.

VII. Who Neutrality Silences

Neutrality invariably silences the already marginalized while legitimizing the already dominant. Voices that challenge institutional legitimacy are often labeled emotional, unprofessional, or divisive. Meanwhile, those defending the status quo are framed as "level-headed" or "nonpartisan." This disparity is not random. It is embedded in platform logic, grant language, and public discourse.

This selective application reveals that the very definition of "balance" and "civility" is often wielded to exclude those whose experiences challenge institutional authority. In 2024, marginalized creators and organizers were disproportionately flagged under content civility codes on LinkedIn and YouTube, especially when naming systems of racialized or economic violence (Sur Journal, 2024). While these moderation rules are framed as fostering discourse, they often suppress critical analysis from those most affected by structural harm. As discussed in previous chapters on platform discipline and NGO framing, who gets silenced is not a bug. It's another built in feature.

VIII. Who This Language Serves

Neutrality is not the absence of ideology. It is the concealment of one. Institutions that insist on neutrality are not disengaged. They are embedded. Their insistence on neutrality is not an objective stance but a reflection of their deep integration within established power structures and the ideologies that sustain them.

Elites like the Gates Foundation, whose public health campaigns frame systemic inequality as "access gaps," or WEF's 2024 "Global Shapers" program, which trains youth leaders to adopt stakeholder language over material critique, benefit directly from this linguistic realignment. Their initiatives are not designed to eliminate conflict. They are designed to manage it. While neutrality is presented as a cornerstone of democracy, it often functions to protect hierarchy from accountability.

You are told neutrality protects fairness. What it protects is power.

The Leash You Voted For

How Consensus Language, Public-Private Partnerships, and Data Alignment Create Voluntary Obedience

I. Soft Control in Plain Sight

Power no longer arrives as command. It arrives as coordination. In the modern control environment, overt coercion is inefficient. Far more effective is a distributed system that wraps behavioral compliance in consensus, wraps consensus in civic language, and wraps civic language in voluntary participation. You are not told what to do. You are offered options. You are nudged toward the one that requires the least resistance.

This structure is not hidden. It is simply not named. ESG scoring, stakeholder capitalism, behavioral nudge systems, and digital trust initiatives are discussed openly in policy memos, foundation reports, and industry panels. These systems promise sustainability, equity, and resilience. What they produce is alignment.

II. ESG as Behavioral Filter

Environmental, Social, and Governance (ESG) scoring began as a framework for corporate accountability. It now functions as a soft sorting mechanism that's used by investors, institutions, and governments to determine which actors are cooperative, compliant, and compatible with global initiatives. ESG data does not measure ethics. It measures harmonization.

In 2024, BlackRock's ESG dashboard began incorporating sentiment data from employee review platforms and social media posts to assess "cultural alignment" (Bloomberg, 2024). Companies whose employees posted labor grievances, climate criticisms, or solidarity with protest movements saw their ESG ratings decline. This isn't malice. It's calibration. ESG is not about what a company stands for. It's about what it can be counted on to tolerate.

III. Stakeholder Capitalism and the Displacement of Politics

Stakeholder capitalism claims to expand corporate responsibility by including workers, communities, and the environment in strategic decisions. In practice, it often displaces democratic accountability with branded consensus. Input is collected, synthesized, and published in corporate impact reports. The structure remains untouched. But the language now includes everyone.

WEF's 2024 resilience index praised stakeholder-led initiatives that "replaced contentious regulatory proposals with community-led adaptation plans." In reality, this meant replacing enforceable protections with informal partnerships. The result is a privatized legitimacy loop: corporations draft the rules, NGOs validate the framing, and governments amplify the narrative. The public is not excluded. It is absorbed.

IV. Public-Private Harmonization

The most effective systems of behavioral control today are neither purely public nor purely private. They are hybrid interfaces, where data, funding, and policy circulate seamlessly between state agencies, multilateral institutions, and corporations. These systems do not require conspiracy. They function through shared incentives.

In 2024, the UNDP's "data resilience" platform integrated inputs from Mastercard, WHO, and Meta to monitor health behavior and economic activity across 22 countries. Governments were encouraged to adopt the platform to "streamline response." Adoption included social media sentiment analysis and mobile metadata tracking. The framing was humanitarian. The effect was standardization. As seen in prior chapters on platform compliance and NGO alignment, the overlap is the control.

V. Voluntary Systems of Obedience

Participation is framed as empowerment. You opt in to health dashboards, school apps, workplace platforms, and resilience networks. But these systems do not simply serve you. They extract, sort, and score you. The price of full participation is legibility.

The Gates Foundation's 2024 "Education Access Toolkit" offered free AI tools to public school systems in low-income districts. Adoption required integration with Microsoft Teams, Google Classroom, and behavioral analytics dashboards. Districts that opted out were deprioritized for future funding. The tools were free. The compliance was not. This pattern echoes the NGO formatting trap and platform audit systems from earlier essays: help is available but only if you ask correctly.

A key enabler of harmonized compliance is the push for universal digital identity. These systems claim to increase access, but their function is alignment. In 2024, the World Economic Forum's "Known Traveler Digital Identity" framework expanded pilot programs in multiple countries, linking biometric data, travel history, and vaccination status to a single profile. Participation remained optional but opting out meant longer waits, fewer permissions, and restricted movement. Digital ID systems don't arrest you. They deny you access. They don't coerce. They incentivize submission through frictionless privilege.

VI. Harmonized Narratives, Sanitized Dissent

Aligned institutions no longer need to silence critique directly. They neutralize it upstream by structuring what is fundable, promotable, or algorithmically compatible. Language becomes the interface. Reports, campaigns, and toolkits use identical phrasing: resilience, impact, sustainability, equity. These words have no fixed content. They serve as credentialing codes.

Dissent that fails to adopt the approved grammar is flagged as unserious. In 2024, climate activists who refused to frame demands as "adaptation strategies" were excluded from COP28 roundtables. Labor groups who named extraction or profit were replaced with "future of work" coalitions. This is not censorship. It is substitution. The radical is replaced with the interoperable. Once-aligned movements now struggle to name their enemy.

Words like "freedom," "justice," and "human rights" have been adopted by the very institutions they once challenged. Semantic capture defangs critique by colonizing its vocabulary. When a surveillance firm talks about "empowerment" or a hedge fund speaks of "equity," the terms lose directional force. Protest becomes branding. Reform becomes a UX upgrade. And without a shared language for opposition, even radical goals are funneled into technocratic deliverables.

VII. Consensus as a Behavioral Architecture

The most powerful systems today do not demand your

submission. They request your input. They convene. They gather. They assess. The process feels democratic. But the outcome is shaped before you arrive. These systems are structured to route dissent into compatible outputs. Your frustration is noted. Your resistance is translated.

In 2024, the World Bank's "Community Listening Labs" piloted public feedback systems in five countries. Responses were pre-categorized into "insight themes" using AI clustering. Phrases like "neoliberal extraction" or "forced displacement" were redirected into "infrastructure equity" and "community integration." Feedback became data. Data became strategy. And participation became proof that the system was working.

VIII. Who This System Serves

This is not the soft tyranny of well-meaning bureaucrats. It is the strategic engineering of compliance through shared language, fused systems, and performative inclusion. The leash is not pulled by force. It is reinforced through incentive, formatting, and automated alignment.

Elites like Klaus Schwab, whose 2024 "Global Resilience Agenda" proposed unified metrics for education, mobility, and institutional trust, do not need to suppress. They orchestrate. Philanthropic giants like the Gates Foundation, and data brokers like Palantir and Meta, function not as separate actors but as linked nodes in an adaptive mesh. The control is not imposed. It is embedded.

You are told this is participation. But what you are participating in is calibration.

The Bilderberg Template

How Private Summits Shape Public Consensus

I. The Illusion of Irrelevance

Bilderberg is not a secret. It is simply not treated as serious. Each year, a rotating group of financial executives, defense officials, media heads, and technocrats meet in private under the pretext of "informal dialogue." There are no minutes, no votes, no official statements. This absence of structure is treated as proof of harmlessness. But that is the design. Bilderberg does not command. It synchronizes. It creates alignment among elite institutions before those institutions ever draft policy or speak to the public.

Like the NGO summits and stakeholder forums covered in earlier chapters, Bilderberg operates in the open but its influence is dismissed as either conspiracy bait or elite leisure. This erasure is functional. While the attendees are undoubtedly powerful, dismissing Bilderberg solely as a social event ignores its role in shaping elite understanding before decisions are made.

II. Who Gets Invited, and Why That Matters

Attendance is selective. Bilderberg does not seek diversity of thought. It curates institutional leverage: central bankers, defense ministers, platform CEOs, senior media executives. Each is invited as a "private individual," but that legal fiction only exists to sever accountability from access. The real function is institutional alignment without the liability of formal negotiation.

While attendees participate ostensibly as individuals, their institutional reach makes the resulting alignment a matter of public concern.

This is not unique. Earlier chapters explored how the same legal fiction shields offshore finance, surveillance contractors, and "independent" research groups from democratic oversight. It is a pattern: separate the actor from the action, then claim deniability.

Bilderberg also functions as a grooming mechanism. Young leaders from finance, tech, or politics are sometimes invited not because they hold power, but because they soon will. Their presence is a preview and a test: are they ideologically flexible? Do they respond to institutional gravity? Attendance signals entry into an unspoken network of shared language and future opportunity. Like Davos's "Young Global Leaders" program, it creates continuity between generations of power, not through doctrine, but through proximity and repetition.

III. Pre-Consensus as Power

Bilderberg's power is not legislative. It is prefigurative. No binding policy emerges. Instead, shared priorities are rehearsed in private, smoothing future convergence. Pre-consensus creates the illusion of independent agreement: policies that later appear across institutions seem spontaneous but actually reflect a harmonized script.

The effect mirrors earlier examples of platform calibration and stakeholder alignment: when powerful actors use different language to deliver the same decisions. While direct causality is difficult to prove, the pattern of convergence across media, banking, tech, and defense demands scrutiny. Agreement does not arise from public debate. It arrives fully formed, dressed in the costume of common sense.

IV. When Discussion Becomes Doctrine

What is floated at Bilderberg frequently becomes embedded elsewhere. "Inclusive growth," "resilience," and "strategic autonomy" were once fringe jargon. After Bilderberg, they migrated to IMF reports, Davos keynotes, and regional development plans. In 2023, "AI risk governance" appeared on the agenda. Within months, major institutions on three continents released frameworks with identical tone and goals: ethical oversight, limited liability, soft compliance.

This is the function of elite pre-consensus: not to enforce doctrine directly, but to make certain ideas inevitable. While these parallel developments could be coincidental, their rhythm, timing, and terminology suggest coordination. The outcome is not imposition but normalization.

V. The Myth of Informality

Bilderberg claims no formal authority. That is the point. There are no minutes to leak, no votes to audit, no resolutions to challenge. But informality is not absence. It is insulation. While Bilderberg lacks binding authority, the alignment achieved among its participants functions as a steering mechanism for institutional behavior.

This is the hallmark of supra-democratic systems: coordination without accountability. A common script emerges not through mandate, but through repetition. The same actors who discuss "trust architecture" at Bilderberg later write white papers, shape policy, and fund research based on that architecture. No enforcement is needed. The script has already been distributed.

Secrecy in the Bilderberg context does not protect sensitive data. It protects structure. By preventing direct attribution, the conference creates a no-liability space where alignment can form without consequence. If a former CIA director, NATO official, and bank CEO all leave with the same vocabulary, there is no trail to contest, only a shift in public rhetoric weeks later. The secrecy is not about hiding plans. It's about obscuring origins. Once consensus is reached, the system will speak with many voices, but one intention.

VI. Media Complicity by Design

Media executives attend Bilderberg. They are not there to report. They are there to align. Bound by the same secrecy rules as other participants, they absorb framing not for exposure, but for replication. This is not an exception. It is the model.

In prior chapters, we examined how media platforms enforce behavioral norms through selective visibility. Bilderberg shifts that upstream. While individual journalists may act with integrity, their editorial directives often reflect consensus formed far above the newsroom. What emerges is not propaganda. It is narrative incubation that's distributed through trusted outlets with no need for central direction.

VII. The Convergence Pattern

There is no need to speculate. The pattern is clear. Discussions at Bilderberg routinely anticipate and then mirror alignment across otherwise unrelated sectors. "Digital sovereignty," "climate adaptation," and "inclusive security" each followed this route: discussed privately, echoed across policy domains, then deployed as if independently developed.

This is not conspiracy. It is elite rehearsal. Like the compliance frameworks and harmonized ESG metrics described later, Bilderberg operates by distributing themes across nodes of power. The ideas are not imposed. They are rehearsed, calibrated, and reintroduced through different institutions with shared timing. While the term "conspiracy" is often used to dismiss such analysis, the observable patterns of elite alignment warrant more serious attention.

VIII. Who This System Serves

Bilderberg does not dictate policy. It predetermines what policy will be considered viable. It does not issue commands. It shapes the terrain on which commands are received. The participants do not govern. They guide the governors. This is not a meeting of individuals. It is a formatting interface for institutional power.

In earlier chapters, we tracked how voluntary participation masks calibrated behavior. Bilderberg extends that model to the apex. You are told this is civic dialogue. What you are witnessing is epistemic closure: elites agreeing on what can be said, what must be avoided, and how to make it all sound reasonable.

They do not need secrecy. They only need coordination. And coordination, at this level, is control.

The World Economic Forum and Preemptive Narrative Management

How the WEF Scripts the Future Before You Debate It

I. The Illusion of Foresight

The World Economic Forum does not predict the future. It scripts it. Through curated white papers, media partnerships, and tightly managed initiatives, the WEF defines which global problems matter, which solutions are "viable," and which stakeholders deserve a seat at the table. These scripts are then echoed by institutions long before the public enters the conversation. This is not reactive forecasting. It is preemptive narrative management: shaping the story before the events unfold.

We've seen this mechanism before, where platforms or NGOs deploy early framing to steer future debate, as in stakeholder models that were "voluntary" until they weren't. While some view the WEF's pronouncements as evidence of visionary insight, their active role in agenda-setting, funding pipelines, and strategic seeding suggests something else: authorship disguised as observation.

II. Who the WEF Actually Serves

The WEF describes itself as an international organization for public-private cooperation, a framing that downplays its actual structure: a membership-based operation in which access, influence, and visibility are contingent on financial buy-in from corporate sponsors. The result is a convergence engine for elite institutions such as banking, technology, defense, and global governance, disguised as a neutral forum.

Despite its claims of neutrality, the WEF's funding model and participant list inherently skew its priorities toward elite continuity. This mirrors earlier chapters on rhetorical camouflage, where organizations project impartiality while operating as coordination hubs for power. What Bilderberg does through informal calibration, the WEF does through glossy reports and press cycles. Both routes lead to the same destination: alignment without democratic input.

III. Script Before Strategy

The Forum does not react to trends. It prefigures them. "The Great Reset," "Fourth Industrial Revolution," and "Stakeholder Capitalism" were all floated at Davos long before they became policy frameworks, grant language, or trade strategy. These were not responses. They were early-stage deployment tools crafted to harmonize public, private, and multilateral action along a single trajectory.

We've tracked this life cycle before: the manufactured consensus that begins with elite language, moves through media repetition, and ends as default policy. While these concepts may gain traction organically over time, their early and coordinated articulation within WEF materials points to a deliberate attempt to steer elite discourse in advance. The convergence is opt-in, but the choices are pre-selected.

The WEF's greatest narrative tool is inevitability. By presenting disruptive technologies, economic restructuring, or social upheaval as "inevitable transformations," the Forum shifts the frame from whether these changes should occur to how best to manage them. This framing disarms critique by repositioning it as denialism. Opposition becomes framed as resistance to progress rather than resistance to privatized control. The trick is simple: decide the future first, then offer managed adaptation as the only rational response.

IV. Davos as a Calibration Hub

Davos is not a summit. It is a staging ground. There are no real negotiations. The panels are not debates. They are performance art. This is where alignment is rehearsed and then displayed for validation. "Cyber resilience," "pandemic preparedness," and "AI governance" each began as WEF reframes before being absorbed into national plans and corporate doctrine. These are not public conversations. They are scripted declarations.

While Davos undoubtedly hosts discussions among powerful figures, its panels are pre-vetted and tightly branded. The goal is not to explore solutions, but to promote convergence. The same ritual played out in NGO grant cycles and ESG impact reports: participation is conditional on tone, phrasing, and alignment. Divergence is not challenged. It is disqualified.

V. Visibility as Legitimacy Theater

Unlike more covert institutions, the WEF leans into visibility. Press kits, white papers, and keynote videos project openness. But the visibility is curated. What is shown is stage lighting. What's hidden is structure. This is not transparency. It is legitimacy theater.

We've already seen how corporate actors use public dashboards and "trust layers" to sanitize extraction. The WEF deploys the same tactic at scale. While it provides a constant stream of public-facing content, the real levers such as partnership deals, regulatory shaping, and agenda scaffolding are conducted out of view. Media partnerships repeat the slogans. The public sees the logo, not the ledger.

VI. Global Governance Without Consent

The WEF holds no office, passes no laws, and issues no mandates. Yet its policy templates, economic models, and governance frameworks ripple outward into trade agreements, central bank guidance, NGO toolkits, and multinational hiring practices. This is governance without representation. The mechanisms are soft. The outcomes are hard.

As detailed in earlier chapters on NGO-proxy enforcement, these structures bypass the public by embedding directives into compliance layers. "Ethical AI" is not a debate. It is a checklist. "Digital trust" is not a demand. It is a credentialing gate. While the WEF claims to offer nonbinding guidance, the adoption of its frameworks without public mandate poses a clear question: if unelected actors can shape the rules, what remains of consent?

One of the WEF's most powerful tools is standardization. It doesn't need enforcement power when its frameworks become the default settings for grants, partnerships, and certifications. From ESG compliance to digital identity protocols, institutions adopt WEF-aligned standards to gain legitimacy, funding, or regulatory favor. Once these templates are embedded, deviation becomes costly. The WEF's influence is not exerted through law but through the creation of a professional environment where only one way of doing things is deemed responsible.

VII. The Doctrine of Manageable Crisis

The WEF does not resolve crisis. It manages it for its own continuity. From climate breakdown to digital destabilization, its initiatives center around controlled instability. The model is not repair. It is *transformation management* with WEF-certified pathways, metrics, and governance structures. The result is constant restructuring under elite supervision.

This is the doctrine of manageable crisis: ensure the world never fully stabilizes, so leadership must remain in the hands of those who claim to understand the chaos. While the WEF presents its work as solution-oriented, its crisis posture guarantees permanent relevance without ever addressing root causes. Every emergency becomes another round of formatting.

We've seen the same logic in platform regulation and resilience discourse. The fire never goes out. It is simply relocated.

VIII. Who This System Serves

The WEF does not forecast. It formats. It does not convene dialogue. It filters it. It does not elevate the global public. It recruits the institutions that will calibrate them. Despite its rhetoric of collaboration, it offers visibility in exchange for compliance and filters out any vision of the future that would destabilize elite networks.

"Narrative preemption" is not an exaggeration. It is the model.

You are told the WEF is a global forum. What it is, in function, is a credentialing system for futures that preserve the current distribution of power. All other futures are discarded before you are ever invited to imagine them.

Think Tanks and War

How Doctrine Becomes Default

I. The Illusion of Independent Thought

Think tanks present themselves as neutral engines of insight. They are not. Most are policy mills, ideological production houses funded by defense contractors, fossil fuel interests, foreign governments, and billionaire foundations. Their job is not to uncover truth. It is to manufacture permission.

While often presented with the veneer of academic rigor, the policy recommendations of think tanks invariably reflect the priorities of their funders and the institutional imperatives of conflict continuity. This mirrors the soft-neutral framing explored in earlier chapters on NGO coordination and research platform calibration. The illusion of independence is tactical. Reports from RAND, CSIS, or the Atlantic Council are received as scholarship, but their output is not neutral. It is strategy, pre-positioned as analysis.

II. How Doctrine Becomes Default

By the time military action becomes a topic of debate, the groundwork has already been laid. Dozens of reports, executive briefs, and policy panels have aligned elite opinion. They frame threats, recommend posture, and define acceptable outcomes. What appears as a natural convergence of political opinion on military action is often the result of a sustained and deliberate intellectual pre-positioning by think tanks.

This pre-consensus model mirrors the elite harmonization described in earlier chapters on WEF narrative seeding and Bilderberg alignment. Escalation does not arrive fully formed. It is built, intellectualized, and absorbed before the public is ever consulted.

III. Strategic Ambiguity as Design

Think tank language is engineered to expand operational freedom while evading accountability. Phrases like "regional stability," "rules-based order," and "responsibility to protect" are not analytical terms. They are linguistic scaffolding, reusable structures that justify intervention under broad pretexts while maintaining rhetorical deniability.

As explored earlier in soft governance and stakeholder policy glossaries, ambiguity is a feature, not a flaw. While some may argue that strategic ambiguity allows for necessary diplomatic flexibility, its primary function in think tank discourse is to broaden the scope for intervention without clear public understanding or consent. When ambiguity defines the premise, escalation can always be justified after the fact.

IV. The Beltway-to-Battlefield Pipeline

Think tanks are not removed from power. They are staffed by it. Retired generals, intelligence officers, and diplomatic staff rotate through these institutions under cosmetic titles such as "fellow," "distinguished chair," and "visiting scholar." These individuals bring not just experience, but continuity. They ensure that doctrine remains unchallenged and that strategic frameworks survive administration changes.

This mirrors earlier critiques of the regulatory-industrial loop, where industry insiders cycle through agencies they once lobbied. While the experience of former officials is undoubtedly valued, their reintegration into think tanks often serves to perpetuate established policy rather than foster critical re-evaluation. The outputs remain consistent because the personnel remain aligned.

V. Foreign Funding, Domestic Outcomes

U.S. foreign policy is shaped not only by domestic institutions but by foreign sponsors who fund the think tanks that inform it. Gulf states, NATO allies, and defense-aligned governments invest heavily in Washington think tanks, using them to shape perceptions of threat, alliance, and response. These institutions then publish reports urging greater military cooperation, arms sales, or permanent troop presence, all in alignment with their sponsors' goals.

As noted in earlier chapters on NGO funding filters, transparency is partial and influence is cumulative. While some funding sources may be disclosed, the extent and influence of foreign contributions on specific policy recommendations often remain opaque to the public. What results is not open dialogue but funded consensus.

VI. Manufactured Consensus

Repetition by multiple think tanks, employing terms like "deterrence posture," "freedom of navigation," and "forward defense," creates a perception of expert consensus. Journalists, politicians, and military officials amplify this language, and through repetition, it solidifies into assumed truth. Alternative frameworks are excluded not through debate, but through omission.

As discussed in earlier critiques of social media feedback loops and corporate PR scripting, consensus is not measured. It is manufactured. While some overlap in language may reflect shared analysis, the coordinated use of specific terms across funded institutions suggests deliberate narrative alignment rather than independent conclusion. The result is harmonized inevitability: a sense that escalation is not a choice, but an obligation.

Think tank outputs do not stay in white papers. They enter headlines. Major outlets often quote reports from institutions like the Brookings Institution, AEI, or RAND without disclosing funding ties or ideological lean. These citations frame the findings as independent expertise. The result is a legitimization loop: think tanks create the narrative, media validates it through repetition, and public officials reference the coverage as justification. What begins as funded strategy ends as presumed fact: an epistemic laundering process where origins are forgotten, but outcomes persist.

VII. The Architecture of the Inevitable

War becomes inevitable not through necessity, but through the slow elimination of alternatives. Think tank frameworks define the problem space. When every report points to containment, forward presence, or deterrence, then deviation is reframed as recklessness. Peace is no longer unwise. It becomes unintelligible.

While think tanks present their recommendations as pragmatic policy options, their underlying function is often to systematically exclude alternatives that do not align with pre-approved frameworks of confrontation. This pattern mirrors earlier chapters where system framing made noncompliance indistinguishable from error. Doctrine, disguised as research, narrows the field until escalation is the only action that still sounds reasonable.

VIII. Who This System Serves

The beneficiaries are known. Defense contractors, security consultants, military logistics firms, and fossil fuel lobbies gain contracts, access, and justification. Policymakers gain cover. Media platforms gain content. The war rationale becomes a closed loop.

As with prior chapters exposing the soft enforcement arms of capital, think tanks function as narrative delivery systems. Their purpose is not to explore all options. It is to collapse the field until only the preferred option remains. While think tanks employ individuals with significant expertise, their structural dependence on vested interests and their role in limiting the scope of policy debate raise serious questions about whose interests this expertise ultimately serves.

They do not inform. They align. And when the narrative work is complete, there is no debate left to have.

The NGO–Intel Feedback Loop

How Humanitarian Fronts Enable Strategic Interventions

I. The Illusion of Neutral Aid

Organizations like USAID, NED, IRI, and Freedom House present themselves as promoters of democracy and development. In practice, they operate as strategic instruments of U.S. foreign policy. Their mission statements center on universal values, but their deployments track closely with geopolitical interests. These are not humanitarian actors. They are formatting agents, civilian instruments used to shape political conditions from within.

This structure mirrors earlier examples of institutional soft power, such as NGO alignment with platform governance or WEF credentialing schemes. While these organizations often frame their work as nonpartisan and apolitical, their embedded role in U.S. strategic operations reveals a more instrumental function. The language is neutral. The effect is directional.

II. Front Channels, Back Objectives

These NGOs fund media outlets, train activists, host civic bootcamps, and distribute toolkits. All are framed as nonpartisan support for civic development. But their activity follows a pattern: support is granted to groups that align with U.S. economic and security goals, while others are ignored or excluded.

This model resembles earlier chapters on stakeholder filtering and grant-based compliance. Just as philanthropic capital shapes acceptable NGO behavior, these democracy promotion programs install Western-style civic systems under the banner of neutrality. Despite being presented as impartial, the strategic targeting and consistent alignment of their activity reveals a deeper purpose: to restructure political process in favor of externally approved outcomes.

III. The Intelligence Partnership

These NGOs are not loosely adjacent to U.S. intelligence services. They are embedded within the same operational framework. NED was created as a "soft" replacement for earlier CIA functions. USAID's Office of Transition Initiatives has operated in tandem with intelligence and defense bodies across dozens of regimes. Staff regularly move between think tanks, embassies, and NGO headquarters.

This fusion echoes previous chapters on public-private harmonization, where boundaries blur between state authority and corporate or civic instruments. While these organizations maintain the appearance of independence, their operational structure reflects a clear strategic alignment. What is portrayed as non-governmental action is often state-directed coordination.

IV. Destabilization as Mandate

These NGOs often enter a country before crisis is visible. When a government is flagged as resistant to Western alignment, these actors begin funding opposition media, advising electoral reform groups, or coordinating protest logistics. In Venezuela, NED-funded outlets were operating years before formal U.S. sanctions intensified. In Eastern Europe, IRI-backed campaigns reframed sovereignty as alignment with NATO and the EU. In Iran, Cuba, and Syria, USAID quietly deployed digital communications tools to circumvent domestic infrastructure.

This is not aid. It is a distributed pressure system. As explored in prior chapters on narrative preloading and elite consensus, the groundwork for conflict is often laid before the public is aware. These NGOs do not merely respond to authoritarian behavior. They help define it in advance, triggering consequences their own actions helped justify.

In many cases, NGO activity helps lay the groundwork for future sanctions or military intervention. Reports generated by "independent" civil society organizations are used in congressional briefings, U.N. resolutions, and media justifications for regime change. These documents often rely on selectively funded sources and pre-aligned metrics. Once cited by government actors, the feedback loop is complete: policy decisions appear to be responding to neutral humanitarian concerns, when in fact those concerns were cultivated to enable the policy. The NGO becomes not a check on power, but its narrative scout.

V. Exporting Protest Templates

These organizations offer standard training in coalition-building, digital strategy, election monitoring, and press engagement. The materials are polished. The outcomes are predictable. The same models appear across continents just translated, reskinned, and aligned with donor expectations.

As previously explored in the chapters on behavioral visibility and compliance scripting, this type of standardized engagement makes dissent legible to external evaluators. While marketed as civic empowerment, the selective provision of resources ensures that only movements compatible with Western strategic aims are amplified. Civil society is not just supported. It is curated.

The playbook doesn't end with protest. NGOs also facilitate the export of post-revolution governance templates: transitional justice systems, economic liberalization programs, public-private partnership frameworks. These packages are rarely neutral. They come embedded with donor-driven economic models and Western regulatory assumptions. In post-uprising environments—from Georgia to Libya—this results in states that may be nominally democratic but remain structurally dependent. The revolution is televised. The rebuilding is outsourced.

VI. The Problem of Plausible Deniability

When NGO-backed campaigns trigger backlash or instability, the state actors funding them retain distance. The organization was independent. The movement was spontaneous. The effect is strategic deniability, which is useful for governments seeking influence without attribution.

This pattern mirrors the use of non-binding frameworks discussed earlier in stakeholder capitalism and ESG scoring. Authority is exerted without accountability. While NGOs contribute to the appearance of organic democratic development, their operating constraints and strategic targeting often place them within a framework of preapproved intervention. The spontaneity is superficial. The outcomes are planned.

VII. Civil Society as a Weaponized Layer

NGOs track opposition groups, fund select campaigns, and elevate voices aligned with foreign policy goals. Protests are not just events. They become metrics. Dissent becomes a data stream. In this system, civil society is transformed into a tactical overlay for strategic influence.

As described in earlier critiques of algorithmic visibility and grant-conditioned resistance, what appears to be grassroots momentum is often formatted in advance. While presented as support for civil society, the tracking and promotion of specific actors serves a second purpose: to convert domestic unrest into leverage. This is not solidarity. It is asset cultivation.

VIII. Who This System Serves

The beneficiaries are strategic planners, multinational investors, aligned platforms, and policy networks seeking compliant regional partners. These NGOs do not merely fund movements. They filter them. What is amplified aligns with strategic frameworks. What resists those frameworks is discarded or defunded.

As with every other system in this book, the offer is framed as help. The outcome is access. These organizations do not promote democracy in general. They format it to fit specific goals. Despite the rhetoric of assistance, the result is a managed civil layer specifically engineered to respond, redirect, or destabilize as needed.

The Price of Rescue

How the IMF and World Bank Enforce Economic Obedience Through Crisis

I. The Illusion of Help

The International Monetary Fund and the World Bank are not neutral helpers. They are enforcement tools, framed as global lifelines but functioning as compliance mechanisms for elite economic order. When nations collapse under debt, disaster, or inflation, the IMF and World Bank arrive. They are not there to restore sovereignty, but to lease it back under supervision.

Like the education toolkits and resilience dashboards examined in earlier chapters, their assistance is offered with pre-written conditions. These are not negotiations. They are formatting devices. While presented as essential for global financial stability and development, the interventions of these institutions often serve to entrench a specific set of models, lock in financial dependencies, and reinforce upstream control. The result is not recovery. It is structured obedience.

II. Conditionality as Command

IMF loans come with structural adjustment programs (SAPs), standardized prescriptions that force countries to privatize, deregulate, cut social services, and open domestic markets to foreign capital. These adjustments are not tailored. They are templated. Like the compliance language embedded in ESG toolkits or NGO grant criteria, their technocratic phrasing conceals an underlying power transaction.

Despite the appearance of consultation, most SAPs operate as ultimatums. The model is binary: accept the package, or collapse. What's framed as partnership is closer to controlled capitulation. These are not adaptive reforms. They are mandates issued through liquidity blackmail.

Compliance isn't enforced by IMF mandates alone. Credit rating agencies, such as Moody's, Fitch, and S&P, reinforce obedience by downgrading noncompliant countries. A nation that resists structural adjustments may find its creditworthiness slashed, triggering capital flight and increased borrowing costs. This forms a secondary pressure circuit: refuse the IMF and lose market access. These agencies appear apolitical, but their evaluations often mirror the same ideological preferences embedded in IMF reforms. Together, they create a coercive environment masked as economic objectivity. No single actor owns the outcome. That is its brilliance. A policy drafted in a think tank, conditioned by IMF lending, and implemented by NGO advisors cannot be traced to a single command. When harm occurs, displacement, austerity, repression, each actor defers responsibility. The report was academic. The loan was optional. The training was nonbinding. In this structure, accountability dissolves at the point of relay. The result is enforcement without fingerprints.

III. Austerity as Economic Weapon

Accepting IMF terms means accepting austerity. The justification is consistent: reduce deficits now to achieve long-term stability. In practice, austerity prioritizes debt servicing and capital flows over social survival. In Greece, the IMF-imposed program shrank GDP by 25 percent and dismantled public services. Argentina's SAPs triggered currency collapse, job loss, and widespread poverty. Ghana's 2023 austerity cuts to education and food subsidies were met with mass protests.

As shown earlier in the rollout of digital governance standards, these policies do not emerge from local need. They are templates, designed to standardize economic regimes for capital access and investor stability. While proponents argue austerity fosters discipline, the historical record reflects stagnation, extraction, and entrenched dependency.

IV. The World Bank's Infrastructure Trap

The World Bank functions under a softer banner of development, but its structure mirrors that of the IMF. It funds large-scale infrastructure projects under poverty-alleviation branding while structuring the returns to benefit external contractors and private capital. Hydropower, transport corridors, and digital grids are financed, but the profits are externalized. The debt remains.

As covered in earlier critiques of public-private partnerships, these projects privatize profits while socializing risk. Governments underwrite the debt. Multinational firms extract the returns. In practice, the infrastructure operates as collateral with functional assets pledged against future control. Despite public branding, the endgame is not sovereign development. It is asset consolidation by foreign actors.

V. Technocracy Without Borders

None of these decisions are made by the populations they affect. IMF and World Bank policies are executed by consultants, economists, and external advisors, professionals accountable to institutions, not to electorates. National budgets are filtered through international templates. Local resistance is dismissed as unsophisticated or irrational.

This pattern reflects what earlier chapters exposed in stakeholder governance systems and multilateral NGO networks: policy displaced from the public sphere into technocratic interface. While defenders of this model point to expertise, its true function is governance without constituency. These systems are not democratic. They are credentialed, exported, and immune to local reversal.

VI. Crisis as Opportunity

Crises accelerate compliance. Whether triggered by natural disaster, pandemic collapse, or capital flight, instability becomes a tool of implementation. The IMF and World Bank offer emergency relief, but the funding is tethered to long-term reforms that would otherwise be politically untenable.

As shown in stakeholder capitalism's post-COVID pivot, crisis formatting permits agenda acceleration. In 2021, pandemic response loans embedded digital identity systems, health platform integration, and fiscal surveillance requirements under humanitarian branding. These were not emergency stopgaps. They were backdoor reforms. The offer was help. The price was structural insertion.

VII. The Two-Tier Sovereignty Model

In wealthy nations, financial failure leads to bailouts, stimulus, and political debate. In the Global South, it leads to external management. Sovereignty becomes contingent, preserved in language, but undermined in operation. National budgets are routed through Washington, Brussels, and Geneva. Local choice is converted into compliance.

This model mirrors earlier critiques of soft governance, where NGO approval, ESG alignment, or stakeholder metrics silently override democratic preference. The IMF and World Bank are not anomalies. They are nodes in the same harmonized system. What was once done with soldiers is now done with spreadsheets and project finance. The logos have changed but the structure has not.

VIII. Who This System Serves

The beneficiaries are not invisible. They are known institutions, such as Western banks, multinational engineering firms, logistics conglomerates, and global consultancies. The IMF ensures creditor repayment. The World Bank ensures private-sector returns. Countries receiving assistance are not rescued. They are processed, sorted, evaluated, and assigned long-term positions within the global debt hierarchy.

As with digital trust systems or ESG filters described earlier, these institutions enforce eligibility through formatting. Nations that comply gain access. Nations that resist are deprioritized. This is not economic aid. It is structured dependency, designed to replicate itself. Debt becomes the interface. Policy becomes the condition.

This is not a rescue. It is a contract. And the repayment plan is written by someone else.

The Control Grid

How Power Consolidates Across Institutions Without a Single Command

I. No Headquarters, No Orders

Power today does not require orders. It requires formatting. The nodes explored in this section, including Bilderberg, the World Economic Forum, the IMF and World Bank, war-policy think tanks, and foreign-funded NGOs, do not compete. They harmonize. They do not require a central authority. They require alignment.

While traditional models of power rely on hierarchy and command, this system achieves consistency through narrative handoff and institutional compatibility. Language shaped at Davos is deployed by RAND and Brookings, then enforced through IMF lending conditions or NGO-backed legitimacy campaigns. Shared incentives obviate the need for directives. Each node knows what its role is, because each is already formatted to interface with the next.

II. From Language to Leverage

Each institution in the grid operates on a different layer, but their actions relay forward. The WEF publishes "future-ready" resilience frameworks. Think tanks like CSIS convert those into policy recommendations. The IMF uses those same benchmarks to condition loans. NGOs echo the language in program metrics and electoral training sessions. The sequence is coherent, even when the institutions are siloed.

While each organization maintains a distinct mission, their work is mutually reinforcing. The system operates not as a unified body but as a policy relay, transferring influence from soft framing to hard enforcement. Language becomes leverage. Empowerment becomes conditioning. Autonomy becomes eligibility. Each node in the system depends on the others to complete its function. The WEF cannot compel adoption of its frameworks without policy codification by think tanks. Think tanks lack enforcement power without financial leverage from lenders. NGOs require upstream justification to secure funding and legitimacy. This interdependence prevents accountability but ensures cohesion. No one institution controls the system, yet none can operate in contradiction to it. The grid is maintained not by command but by the mutual survival of its parts.

III. Consent Through Absence

This model of control does not rely on overt coercion. It relies on filtering. By the time the public engages with an issue, be it digital infrastructure, fiscal restructuring, foreign intervention, or civic unrest, the field of acceptable positions has already been narrowed. Reports have been published. Funding has been pre-allocated. Resistance that falls outside approved frameworks becomes illegible.

While individuals may perceive themselves as making free choices within democratic systems, the surrounding architecture of information, incentives, and constraints has already been shaped. This system does not demand obedience. It deletes the conditions that make disobedience thinkable. Narrative constraint replaces force. When the only futures being modeled, funded, and broadcast are those that align with elite continuity, disagreement is reframed as ignorance. Radical alternatives aren't debated, they're disqualified by omission. Just as previous chapters exposed language gating in stakeholder governance and media scripting, this system disciplines thought before it reaches expression. What survives the filter appears natural. What challenges it disappears as noise.

IV. Who This Grid Serves

Despite branding themselves as stewards of democracy, development, and progress, these institutions operate to protect the continuity of elite power. Bilderberg maintains epistemic alignment. WEF credentializes global frameworks. Think tanks secure ideological discipline. The IMF and World Bank enforce fiscal compliance. NGOs destabilize or reformat opposition as needed.

The beneficiaries are consistent: multinational finance, arms contractors, energy conglomerates, regime-aligned tech platforms, and the planners who broker state alignment through civilian fronts. These systems do not simply fail to serve the public. They are engineered not to.

What results is not tyranny. It is management. Not a dictatorship of force, but a soft mesh of obligations, filters, and credentialed pressure directly structured to ensure that disruption remains unlikely, alternatives remain invisible, and compliance appears voluntary.

Big Tech as Policy Architects

How Google, Amazon, and Meta Build Systems Governments Then Adopt

I. The Illusion of Innovation

Big Tech platforms are framed as innovative, neutral tools that are designed for efficiency and scale. But certain core functions now operate as upstream control systems. Google's search algorithms shape electoral visibility and public memory. Amazon's logistics networks structure access to essential goods, including government supply chains. Meta controls how identity and social legitimacy are established online. These are not just tools. They are inputs into public life, treated as infrastructure before being debated as policy.

Not every product feature implies governance. But content moderation, algorithmic visibility, and backend integration into public systems extend beyond service. They act as soft architectures of authority. The public interacts with these systems as citizens, but they were not designed with democratic oversight in mind.

II. From Product to Protocol

Once adopted by public institutions, platforms transition from products to protocols. Google Workspace governs access in public school districts. AWS runs cloud architecture for local agencies, defense bodies, and public health systems. Meta APIs authenticate users across services, from journalism to civic portals. These systems are often adopted during moments of urgency, cemented through ease and cost. For instance, during the 2020 pandemic, school districts rushed to adopt Google Workspace to enable remote learning, locking in long-term dependence.

While marketed as efficient tools, platforms embed governance rules. AWS formats determine how government data is stored. Meta's content gating dictates what appears in political newsfeeds. These policy scaffolds, pre-installed frameworks that shape public behavior, create compliance by design, not decree.

III. Platform Standards Become Law

Private rules have become behavioral mandates. Terms of service now function as codes of conduct. Algorithms decide visibility. Moderation decisions determine acceptable speech. Supra-democratic control refers to systems, like Meta's election frameworks or YouTube's health panels, that impose public-facing rules without democratic input or appeal.

As we saw earlier with ESG frameworks dictating corporate behavior, private standards can bypass democratic scrutiny entirely. Big Tech's moderation systems operate the same way, by creating invisible rule sets that shape discourse without triggering public debate. These are not law. They are law's substitute.

Soft censorship no longer requires removal. It operates through ranking, delay, and context. Search results are reordered. Posts are "demoted" or shadowbanned. Content is allowed but made hard to find. These actions are enforced by interoperability agreements between platforms and governments, especially during elections or emergencies. While appearing voluntary, they establish enforcement pathways that operate outside courts, law, or public scrutiny. What is visible is no longer decided in public forums. It is adjusted at the code layer.

IV. Ghostwriting the Public Sector

Big Tech does not wait for regulation. It prewrites it. Amazon authors cloud security protocols adopted by federal agencies. Google's AI ethics papers shape international policy drafts. Meta funds and staffs election integrity panels, then incorporates their findings into platform governance. These are not consultations. They are insertions of private frameworks into public rulemaking.

By placing former executives in regulatory roles, platforms like Google ensure their frameworks (such as AI guidelines) are prioritized. Like the think tanks scripting military consensus, or the NGOs formatting acceptable opposition, these companies shape the field before policy is debated. Influence arrives as code, whitepapers, and "best practice."

Tech's dominance is not limited to one sector. It is achieved through multi-domain embedding like education, health, logistics, finance, and defense. These all ensure that resistance in one area is constrained by dependence in another. A regulator may seek to limit data collection, but rely on the same company's cloud infrastructure. A school may object to surveillance, but need Google's learning tools. This interlock strategy mirrors prior chapters on cross-institutional formatting: policy can't diverge if all roads lead back to the same gatekeepers.

V. Policy by Infrastructure

Once adopted, platforms lock institutions into operational dependencies. Palantir's predictive policing dashboards limit what local governments can measure and respond to. AWS governs storage formats and access protocols for state data. Google's tools determine how students submit work, or how health workers exchange data. Meta enforces election speech norms through back-end visibility tools.

Whether by design or effect, these systems precondition behavior. Policy becomes a justification, not a generator. A mayor may still propose reforms, but the dashboard already decided which metrics exist. What is measurable becomes what is actionable. One feature of infrastructural control is deniability. When a school suspends a student based on Google's flagged content, or when a municipality restricts speech on a Meta-integrated forum, blame falls on the institution but not the platform that set the rule conditions. This decoupling of action from authorship creates an ecosystem where private systems govern public life without absorbing responsibility. Platforms shape the choices available, then step aside as institutions enforce them. Regulation is deflected. Accountability is laundered.

VI. The Collapse of Regulation

Regulation fails most often not due to will, but because the systems it seeks to control are already embedded. Governments depend on AWS. Schools rely on Google. Courts accept Facebook data as social proof. While antitrust cases and data laws exist, like the EU's GDPR, the DOJ's Google lawsuit, and the Digital Markets Act, they arrive long after platforms achieve dominance.

Like we saw with the IMF's structural adjustment programs, Big Tech's systems create locked dependencies that reshape the space before enforcement is possible. While regulations like the Digital Markets Act aim to curb platform power, their impact is constrained by public reliance on the very systems they attempt to regulate.

VII. Digital Feudalism

Platforms now operate as lords over digital territories. Amazon governs logistics. Google governs visibility. Meta governs identity. Institutions rent access. Users lease functionality. Public life is reconstructed inside proprietary environments with no exit ramp.

Digital feudalism describes a system in which Big Tech offers the conditions of participation in exchange for data, conformity, and continued tenancy. Users may choose platforms for convenience, but this is a false choice when alternatives like Mastodon or Proton are excluded, starved of reach, or acquired, as Meta did with WhatsApp. Open protocols exist. They are simply nonviable at scale because the platforms that dominate the space also gate its discoverability.

VIII. Who This System Serves

The beneficiaries are not the users. They are monopolists, predictive policing vendors, regulatory consultants, state partners, and institutional investors. The platform model does not build civic capacity. It absorbs it and then sells it back as service.

Like the NGOs and think tanks in earlier chapters, Big Tech's power lies in upstream design. It scripts outcomes before public debate occurs. The infrastructure becomes the law. As further chapters will explore, this privatized authority now merges with financial surveillance systems to create a seamless enclosure of public behavior. Upstream design is not a technical choice. It is a political weapon.

The Surveillance Web

How Fusion Centers, Data Brokers, and Platform Partnerships Built a Domestic Intelligence Apparatus

I. The Myth of Post-9/11 Reform

After 9/11, the U.S. public was told that expanded surveillance was a temporary necessity. The Patriot Act, FISA amendments, and DHS's counterterrorism buildout were introduced as emergency tools to prevent foreign attacks. But key surveillance mechanisms, especially fusion centers and digital intelligence partnerships, quietly turned inward. They became permanent domestic fixtures, despite occasional legal pushback, such as FISA court reforms.

While proponents argue surveillance prevents terrorism, its scope expanded to cover protest movements, journalists, and civic organizers. Fusion center bulletins on Occupy Wall Street, Black Lives Matter, and Keystone Pipeline protests illustrate how visibility became risk. The targets were not foreign actors. They were domestic friction points.

II. Fusion Centers as Domestic Surveillance Hubs

Today, more than 80 federally linked fusion centers operate across the United States. Funded by DHS and staffed with agents from the FBI, ICE, state police, and private contractors, these centers function as domestic intelligence hubs. They aggregate camera feeds, license plate scans, social media scraping, financial transactions, and biometric data. The system's purpose is not prosecution. It is continuous monitoring.

For example, the Boston Regional Intelligence Center tracked climate activists using social media data prior to demonstrations. Similarly, Muslim community centers have been flagged in threat assessment reports for "pattern deviations." These actions were framed as "suspicious activity," despite a lack of criminal conduct. Coordination becomes profiling. Normal behavior becomes anomaly.

Fusion centers operate in a gray zone where they are not fully law enforcement, not fully intelligence. The result is a para-intelligence culture, where analysts generate "threat assessments" with no clear evidentiary burden. These assessments are shared across jurisdictions, uploaded into interagency portals, and used to flag individuals who may never be charged with a crime. Once labeled as a concern, a person's name can persist across systems for years. There is no appeals process. The logic mirrors systems described earlier: upstream filters that embed suspicion into institutional memory without accountability.

III. Big Tech as Voluntary Informant

Tech platforms are not passive participants. They actively develop tools law enforcement now uses natively. Google's geofence API allows police to request all user data within a defined physical boundary. Amazon's Rekognition matches faces in real-time from public video streams. Meta shares moderation records and metadata to assist in behavioral mapping.

Though companies claim to comply with law, their voluntary development of tools like Rekognition and geofence analytics extends well beyond what courts mandate. Google provided geofence data in Capitol riot investigations, despite no blanket legal requirement to collect or structure it that way. As Chapter 3 showed with ESG frameworks dictating corporate compliance without voter input, Big Tech enables state surveillance under the guise of convenience. These features are not passive. They are prepositioned.

IV. Data Brokers and the Legal Bypass

Much of today's surveillance is not judicial. It is contractual. Data brokers compile app usage, GPS pings, purchasing history, and browsing data, then sell it to government agencies without warrants. While data brokers cite compliance with weak consumer protection laws, their sale of sensitive data, like Venntel's location tracking feeds to ICE, bypasses robust Fourth Amendment scrutiny.

Not all broker activity is unconstitutional. Some vendors operate within existing legal bounds, such as selling public records. But the system's core value is in selling access to information that would otherwise require legal thresholds. This is not regulatory loopholing. It is structural delegation. State actors acquire what courts would deny simply by buying it.

V. Financial and Behavioral Integration

Fusion centers increasingly integrate behavioral data with financial surveillance. Institutions like Palantir connect social signals with spending patterns, location movements, and communication metadata. Their Gotham platform, for instance, flags deviation from statistical baselines, as seen in ICE operations targeting immigrant populations.

Like the IMF's risk-based lending seen earlier, which penalized economic deviation, fusion centers treat behavioral outliers as threats to be preemptively contained. What was once public space is now eligibility space. Compliance is not demanded. It is modeled and scored. If you deviate, you are flagged. If you match, you pass.

VI. The Construction of Suspicion

Surveillance no longer waits for evidence. It assigns potential. Categories like "pre-incident behavior" and "threat architecture" reframe activity as future risk. For targeted groups like activists and journalists, visibility often becomes liability, as seen in DHS monitoring of Black Lives Matter protests and climate justice coalitions.

This does not mean all dissent is punished. Resources are finite. The system is selective. But its structure permits indiscriminate flagging and its logic is replicable. When data is abstracted from behavior, and behavior is judged by potential risk, public presence becomes a variable of interest. Suspicion becomes ambient.

VII. No Court, No Consent

Fusion centers operate outside traditional legal frameworks. Their inputs are aggregated from vendors, not subpoenas. Their assessments are generated by private software. Their thresholds are internally defined. There is no trial. There is no hearing. The subject is not notified. The record is not expunged.

Upstream design, seen in platform architecture and NGO frameworks, allows fusion centers to embed surveillance before public debate can occur. Like Big Tech's systems, they operate before you know the rules exist. Governance happens before law.

Control is infrastructural, not procedural.

Once flagged, individuals often remain in fusion center records indefinitely. These entries can affect employment screenings, security clearances, or interagency referrals, even when no crime was committed. Unlike criminal records, which can sometimes be expunged, fusion center data has no public redress pathway. It's not illegal, it's just unofficial. But in systems of diffuse control, unofficial status is enough. You don't have to be guilty. You only have to be tagged.

VIII. Who This System Serves

This system serves predictive analytics vendors, private surveillance contractors, federal grants recipients, and law enforcement networks seeking compliance without conflict. It serves elite institutions that prefer data-driven intervention to political response. It does not protect the public. It manages the public.

As we will explore later, this surveillance web integrates with digital currency systems and centralized identity verification to enforce compliance through financial and behavioral control. This is not a network of threats. It is a system of formatting that was built to detect, correct, and sort behavior before resistance can form.

The Black Budget State

How Classified Programs Outlive Oversight and Evade Reform

I. The Illusion of Temporary Powers

Every era of emergency leaves behind permanent tools. The Cold War justified mass surveillance. The War on Drugs enabled civil asset forfeiture and militarized policing. The War on Terror normalized warrantless wiretaps, predictive flagging, and extrajudicial detention. While some powers have faced legal challenges, such as the rollback of certain asset forfeiture provisions in states like New Mexico, key surveillance tools persist by redefining their targets.

Classified programs do not sunset. They ossify. Powers granted to stop foreign adversaries are repurposed to monitor journalists, dissidents, and political organizers. NSA's PRISM program, initially justified as a counterterrorism measure, continued long after 9/11 to collect domestic metadata. While advocates argue these programs protect against terrorism, their persistence in targeting domestic dissent, like COINTELPRO's surveillance of civil rights groups, prioritizes continuity and control over public safety.

II. Black Budgets and Shadow Networks

The U.S. now spends over $80 billion annually on its classified intelligence budget, excluding covert allocations embedded in defense contracts or nontransparent agency accounts. These funds are shielded from public and congressional scrutiny. Legislators are briefed on top-line figures, not granular allocations.

Funds are channeled through classified appropriations, like the CIA's discretionary accounts, which bypass detailed committee review. Like the IMF's lending conditions in Chapter 4, which enforce compliance without voter input, black budgets ensure operational autonomy without public scrutiny. The purpose is not misappropriation. It is insulation. These are not rogue programs. They are sovereign systems inside the state.

III. Compartmentalization as Strategy

Within the classified ecosystem, information is deliberately fractured. Programs are subdivided and access is granted only through rigid clearance hierarchies. Fragmentation, enforced through strict clearance protocols, ensures that even senior officials lack the full picture. Congressional oversight committees have been denied access to entire NSA programs under "need-to-know" exceptions.

This structure produces deniability through ignorance. A senator may fund a system they cannot audit. A contractor may execute a protocol they do not understand. This is not deception. It is protocol. Compartmentalization prevents leaks but also accountability.

IV. Contractor Control and Revolving Doors

Most classified programs are built and maintained by private firms. Booz Allen Hamilton, Palantir, Raytheon, and Lockheed Martin develop data analytics tools, maintain intelligence platforms, and manage signal capture infrastructure. These firms do not just fulfill contracts. They help define them.

While contractors face nominal regulation, their self-drafted protocols, like Palantir's predictive policing algorithms, often evade rigorous external review due to classified exemptions. Contractors like Palantir often draft compliance frameworks with minimal external review, enabling self-regulated surveillance. This creates a revolving door: a former NSA official joins a defense firm. A private analyst moves into a federal advisory role. Like ESG consultants who write the same impact rubrics they later score, accountability is absorbed into continuity.

V. Legacy Programs That Persist

Classified systems do not retire. They mutate. ECHELON, the Cold War-era communications dragnet, was never dismantled. Its functions were absorbed into NSA metadata programs and partner networks like Five Eyes. COINTELPRO's domestic surveillance strategy reemerged in fusion center bulletins targeting environmental and racial justice protestors. Continuity of Government (COG) protocols which were originally written for nuclear war are still funded and periodically drilled.

COG refers to classified plans for preserving state function during national emergencies. Today, they are used to justify ongoing surveillance and emergency continuity powers. Programs like COINTELPRO mutate by repurposing tools for new targets, driven by bureaucratic inertia and flexible threat definitions. As Chapter 6 showed with fusion centers targeting protestors, these systems persist by adapting to new forms of dissent.

In black budget systems, longevity is not a side effect. It's the goal. Once embedded, programs develop bureaucratic momentum.

They generate their own justifications, renewal cycles, and threat assessments. Every review process depends on insiders, who benefit from continuation. When programs mutate, they do so laterally, adopting new targets or terminologies to stay relevant. The result is a governance layer that evolves without public mandate, insulated by its own procedural gravity.

VI. The Legal Firewall

Classified programs are legally fortified. Executive orders, intelligence exemptions, and national security doctrines shield them from FOIA requests, public litigation, and most journalistic scrutiny. Courts do not review the content of black programs. They review the justification for secrecy. Oversight committees receive summaries but rarely source material.

Classified briefings are cited as oversight, but their restricted scope, as seen in limited disclosures about NSA's PRISM operations, prevents meaningful control. This firewall is not accidental. It is procedural. Like data brokers who bypass Fourth Amendment review through private contracts, classified systems treat law as a boundary to be avoided, not a system to operate within.

Black programs do not just hide information. They manage perception. Public awareness of their existence is often confined to leaks, whistleblower disclosures, or redacted fragments. This partial visibility creates a paradox: the public is vaguely aware of classified powers, but lacks specifics to contest them. The effect is preemptive resignation. You cannot fight what you cannot describe. The law's opacity becomes a psychological filter causing suspicion without evidence and concern without leverage.

VII. Beyond Elections

Democratic elections do not alter black program trajectory. Presidents may change but the agencies remain. Classified directives outlive administrations. Funding priorities continue uninterrupted. While elections may shift rhetoric or prompt minor reforms, such as post-Snowden encryption protocols, the infrastructure of classified programs remains largely untouched, insulated by continuity doctrines.

Elections may change the face of leadership. But like Big Tech platforms or IMF lending, the system operates through embedded control, not voter input. What appears as change is often surface rotation. The architecture does not respond to the ballot box.

VIII. Who This System Serves

This architecture serves intelligence contractors, military-industrial lobbies, federal continuity planners, and elite actors who require governance without interference. These systems do not exist to respond. They exist to outlast.

As later chapters will explore, these classified budgets increasingly fund digital identity and financial surveillance systems, embedding control deeper into public life. Like the upstream design of Big Tech platforms, black budget programs preinstall authority by shaping outcomes before democratic input can occur. These are not hidden systems. They are governing ones. What you see is elective. What rules is not.

Continuity of Government (COG)

How Emergency Protocols Became Permanent Mechanisms for Domestic Control

I. The Myth of Dormant Protocols

Continuity of Government (COG) is widely believed to be a Cold War contingency that is activated only in the face of nuclear war or existential collapse. This framing is outdated. While COG is justified as essential for government survival, its use in peacetime crises, like the 2020 protest response and pandemic planning, prioritizes control over democratic function.

Key protocols have not remained dormant. They have been revised, funded, and integrated into crisis logistics for terrorism, pandemics, cyberattacks, and mass unrest. What began as nuclear fallback has evolved into continuity planning for everyday disruption. These systems are not emergency backups. They are standby governance.

II. What COG Actually Includes

COG protocols include executive succession plans, relocation logistics, crisis communications overrides, and presidential emergency action documents (PEADs), which are classified executive orders that authorize suspension of habeas corpus, domestic detention without trial, and rapid reorganization of federal authority.

Facilities like Mount Weather and Raven Rock are not abandoned bunkers. They are maintained relocation sites, with secure communication networks and pre-scripted authority handoffs. COG tools, like PEADs, are integrated into peacetime systems through classified exercises, such as FEMA's 2020 pandemic drills, which tested domestic control measures. These tools are not hypothetical. They are operational.

III. Authority Without Transparency

COG can be activated by executive directive, with no public notification or congressional vote. Oversight committees, like the Senate Intelligence Committee, are routinely denied full PEAD details due to classified restrictions, as seen in post-9/11 briefings. Even elected officials operate on a need-to-know basis.

Like the black budget compartmentalization in Chapter 8, COG's fragmented information shields core directives from scrutiny. The result is centralized power under conditions of manufactured ignorance. The rules are secret. The system is active. The voter has no jurisdiction over either.

IV. From Wartime to Everything Time

COG's justifications have expanded from nuclear war to include vague "national continuity risks," like pandemics or protests, enabling domestic applications, as seen in 2020 continuity exercises. The term "national continuity risk" refers to threats broadly defined by internal security agencies, including natural disasters, cyberattacks, and civil unrest.

Though COG is portrayed as a rare contingency, its frequent activation, such as in FEMA's pandemic and civil unrest drills, shows it as a routine tool for domestic management. These are not wartime systems adapted to modern crises. They are governance protocols looking for justification.

V. Peacetime Rehearsals

COG systems are tested regularly through classified continuity exercises. The National Continuity Coordinator oversees multi-agency rehearsals like Eagle Horizon, which simulate crisis response, chain-of-command transfer, and infrastructure lockdown. These drills are not passive. They refine active readiness.

Drills like Eagle Horizon normalize COG protocols by embedding them in agency workflows, as seen when FEMA tested continuity plans during 2020 protests, shaping real-time crisis response. As we saw with Big Tech's platform protocols shaping policy, COG drills embed control before public input. What gets rehearsed becomes the default.

VI. Contractors and Private Command

Contractors manage critical functions of the COG ecosystem. Firms like Booz Allen Hamilton, Leidos, and SAIC write continuity software, simulate scenario planning, and build crisis infrastructure. While contractors face nominal oversight, their classified COG contracts, such as continuity software development, evade public scrutiny due to national security exemptions. This mirrors the privatized control structures we examined earlier. Outsourced governance becomes upstream engineering. The vendor writes the rules, installs the system, and then certifies compliance under its own terms. Public sovereignty is replaced by sealed procurement.

VII. Pre-Installed Governance

Certain COG protocols, like PEADs authorizing detention without trial, function as pre-installed martial law that is ready to override democratic norms under classified triggers. These rules exist whether the public consents or not. Elections do not review them. Congress cannot revoke what it cannot read.

Upstream control, seen in earlier platform architecture and surveillance web, defines COG's power to preinstall governance before democratic debate. The system is not paused when crisis hits. It is activated. The government that emerges is not the one voters chose. It is the one planners designed.

VIII. Who This System Serves

COG ensures institutional survival, but it also safeguards elite control. It guarantees continuity for contractors, federal planners, and national security officials regardless of political upheaval. In crises like mass unrest, as seen in post-9/11 continuity activations, COG enables elites to inherit control while public input is suspended.

As we will explore, COG's pre-installed control converges with digital currency systems and identity surveillance to enforce compliance through crisis triggers. This is not about what happens when government collapses. It is about what happens when democracy does. The replacement is already built. The transition is automatic.

CBDCs as Financial Fencing

How Central Bank Digital Currencies Enable Spend-Tracking and Economic Behavior Enforcement

I. The Illusion of Modernization

Central Bank Digital Currencies (CBDCs) are marketed as the next step in monetary efficiency for being secure, programmable, and inclusive. They promise easier welfare disbursement, reduced fraud, and low-cost payments. But many CBDCs, particularly in major economies like China and the EU, are centralized by design, embedding conditions, surveillance, and override mechanisms, as seen in China's digital yuan trials and the European Central Bank's digital euro proposals.

While CBDCs are touted for financial inclusion, their surveillance and restrictions, such as China's limits on welfare recipients' spending categories, prioritize control over access. Unlike decentralized cryptocurrencies or physical cash, CBDCs are issued and tracked by the state. Their promise is not modernization. It is interface-level governance.

CBDCs are often promoted alongside the quiet phaseout of physical cash. Pilot programs in Sweden and Nigeria have coincided with ATM closures, merchant cash refusal, and the erosion of anonymous payment options. As cash becomes functionally obsolete, participation in a tracked system becomes mandatory by default. This transition is framed as progress, but its true effect is to eliminate the last form of unmediated economic freedom. When no alternative exists, consent is implied, whether given or not.

II. Programmability and Spend-Conditioning

CBDCs are programmable units. Governments, as in China's digital yuan pilot, program restrictions through central bank APIs, blocking transactions based on predefined rules like location or product type. This allows real-time enforcement: a token may expire after 30 days, fail outside a designated zone, or be disabled for certain purchases.

This is not theory. It is already being tested. A "green wallet" might block air travel or meat during a climate campaign. An "emergency wallet" might lock transfers during protest activity. Programmability turns currency into a policy enforcement tool, not by criminalizing action, but by removing liquidity. You are not punished. You are simply blocked.

III. Financial Visibility as Total Access

Every CBDC transaction is logged. When integrated with mobile geolocation, digital ID, and social platforms, as in China's WeChat ecosystem, CBDC use creates a live spending graph: a behavioral model derived from payment patterns. For instance, China's digital yuan integrates transaction data with WeChat's social graph, creating behavioral profiles that flag dissent, such as donations to protest organizations.

As our look at the surveillance web showed with fusion centers flagging activists, CBDCs extend visibility into financial behavior. The state no longer needs to ask what you believe. It sees what you fund. The transaction is not just a log. It is a signal.

IV. Eligibility Scoring and Transaction Gating

In systems like China's digital yuan, CBDCs enable enforcement by making dissent unaffordable, linking transactions to social credit or protest data. A flagged user might be unable to book transportation, donate to organizations, or access subsidies. There is no trial. There is only ineligibility.

Like IMF lending criteria conditioning aid on compliance, CBDCs gate transactions based on behavioral scores. This is not prohibition. It is quiet exclusion. You are not told you cannot act. You are told you are ineligible to pay.

V. Emergency Triggers and System Overrides

CBDCs can be suspended, narrowed, or redirected under emergency orders. Emergencies, in turn, are defined internally. Central banks, as in the ECB's digital euro framework, define emergencies like "public trust erosion" through internal risk metrics, enabling overrides such as account freezes or withdrawal limits.

This mirrors Continuity of Government protocols, where the same authority that defines crisis also activates extrajudicial control. The override is not reactive. It is pre-installed. The wallet fails. The user receives no explanation.

VI. Partner Institutions and Corporate Alignment

CBDCs will not be enforced directly by central banks. They will be administered through private platforms such as banks, vendors, and apps that integrate central bank APIs. While private platforms enforce CBDC rules, as Visa does with compliance APIs, they act under state-defined parameters, as seen in China's central bank mandates to vendors and payment gateways.

As we've already seen, this public-private fusion allows policy to be enacted without legislation. Rule enforcement migrates to code. Governance migrates to infrastructure.

VII. From Currency to Control Layer

CBDCs can turn key actions like donations, subscriptions, or peer-to-peer transfers into compliance levers by linking them to behavioral data, as seen in China's trials blocking flagged accounts. The result is not a new payment method. It is a silent eligibility gate for public participation.

Cash is autonomy. CBDCs are contingent access. You are not told what you may not do. You are told what you cannot afford. The refusal is invisible. The denial is automatic.

VIII. Who This System Serves

CBDCs serve central banks, compliance vendors, surveillance regulators, and any institution that benefits from downstream enforcement without upstream debate. They allow governments to shape markets, suppress dissent, and enforce policies through liquidity, without legislation or confrontation.

As we will explore, CBDCs integrate with global financial surveillance and digital identity systems to create a seamless control grid. Upstream control, seen in platform architecture and COG protocols, defines CBDCs' power to preinstall compliance before democratic input. This is not financial modernization. It is perimeter design. You are not told you are trapped. You are simply unable to exit.

Opting out of Existence

How Infrastructure Became the Interface for Behavioral Control

I. From Opt-In Tools to Embedded Rule Sets

Infrastructure no longer presents itself as an optional interface; it now defines the boundaries within which modern life operates. Across the systems examined in this section, which include Big Tech platforms, fused surveillance data, legacy black programs, continuity governance protocols, and central bank digital currencies, the shift is consistent: rules are no longer passed down through policy debates or visible enforcement. They are embedded in the tools themselves, quietly formatting the user's range of motion without ever requiring announcement.

Infrastructure, like the digital yuan with built-in spending limits, preserves the appearance of user agency through familiar interfaces, even as it predefines acceptable behavior beneath the surface. As we have previously illustrated, these systems do not remove options by prohibition, they remove them from the menu before the user even arrives.

II. What You Cannot Opt Out Of

In many modern jurisdictions, the possibility of meaningful opt-out has largely collapsed. Countries like Sweden, where physical cash has nearly vanished from circulation, leave users with little practical alternative to state-sanctioned digital payment systems. In the United States, fusion centers routinely share behavioral data with financial institutions, making anonymous transactions virtually impossible. Continuity of Government (COG) protocols, once reserved for nuclear war, now sit in the background of democratic governance, capable of quietly overriding electoral outcomes under classified emergency conditions. Meanwhile, China's rollout of the digital yuan enforces CBDC use in pilot regions, conditioning access to basic services on participation in the centralized currency system.

While theoretical alternatives exist, such as cryptocurrencies, local barter systems, and cash reserves, their systemic marginalization through platform delisting, exchange restrictions, and legal pressure ensures that they remain inaccessible to most users under conditions of urgency. As we established, this isn't coercion by force; it is exclusion through credential failure.

III. The Architecture of Preemption

Increasingly, these systems do not wait for problematic behavior to emerge; they act based on predictive signals derived from past data and inferred risk. In authoritarian environments like China's social credit system or in domestic intelligence structures such as U.S. fusion centers, threat designation now occurs long before any formal violation has taken place. While legal mechanisms such as GDPR occasionally slow or restrict the reach of such preemption, the trend is clear: dissent is not confronted; it is routed around.

As demonstrated earlier, the mere association with targeted ideas, flagged keywords, or anomalous patterns can trigger denial. Preemption doesn't require prohibition. It simply removes the logistical possibility of organizing, transferring funds, or accessing tools. The systems never declare an objection. They disable the opportunity.

IV. Control Without Announcement

Whereas traditional repression relies on visible enforcement such as arrests, bans, and censorship, these infrastructural systems control without spectacle. Service degradation, account suspensions, and quiet debanking do not resemble coercion. They appear as friction. They register as error messages, login failures, or unexplained freezes.

Mechanisms like Palantir's predictive policing tools or Meta's content moderation engines translate behavioral flags into functional denials, automating eligibility decisions through probabilistic models. As documented earlier, protestors have found their payment apps locked without warning. These are not policy decisions debated in public. They are backend routines executing in real time.

Efforts to resist from within these infrastructures are often formatted in advance. Appeals systems, complaint forms, and oversight bodies exist but they are designed to absorb frustration, not reverse outcomes. Most rely on opaque algorithms, vague terms of service, or unreviewable risk protocols. By offering channels for redress that rarely function, the system simulates accountability without permitting disruption. Resistance becomes a UI feature. The rage is recorded. The rules remain.

V. System Interlock by Design

The appearance of separation between these domains, including finance, mobility, identity, and governance, is increasingly misleading. In China, the integration of CBDCs, surveillance feeds, and social credit scoring provides a clear model of convergence, where data circulates seamlessly through multiple enforcement layers. Western systems, though less overt, are moving in the same direction. In the U.S., financial institutions are now active participants in national security screening, sharing customer behavior with law enforcement through formal data agreements.

These linkages enable behaviors flagged in one domain to produce cascading effects in others. A donation to a blacklisted group may not trigger arrest, but it can result in financial throttling, travel restriction, or reputational suppression across platforms. What appears to be separate systems instead act in concert. The gate does not close in one place. It closes everywhere at once.

As systems interlock, individuals cease to be treated as citizens with rights and instead become data subjects with risk scores. Identity becomes transactional and validated only through continuous compliance across interfaces. A person whose financial, social, or mobility credentials are flagged in one system may find their digital identity shadowbanned across many. What results is not loss of status, but erasure by filtration: the individual remains present, but unrecognized by the systems that confer access.

VI. Stability as Policy, Not Outcome

What binds these systems is not a shared ideology, but a shared function: the maintenance of uninterrupted operation. Predictive surveillance frameworks exist to prevent social disruption before it manifests. COG systems are structured to guarantee executive continuity in the face of democratic instability. CBDCs are designed not merely to facilitate transactions, but to preserve monetary control through behavioral compliance. Platform content moderation increasingly serves to stabilize narrative cohesion, regardless of whether public consensus exists.

As seen with IMF policy enforcement, and again in classified continuity programs, the consistent priority across these systems is not legitimacy but uptime. The system remains in motion, even when the public no longer moves it.

Even visibility is no longer guaranteed. Accounts can be throttled without deletion, voices suppressed without bans. What you say may not be censored but it may simply fail to propagate. Eligibility for reach, recommendation, or access is contingent on alignment. Like digital credit scoring or NGO credential filters, visibility now functions as a gate. To be seen is no longer a right. It is a conditional state, granted only to those who do not disrupt the machine that sees them.

In this model, traditional institutions like courts, legislatures, media, and protest spaces still exist, but their functional relevance erodes. They serve as legacy rituals that simulate input while real enforcement has migrated to infrastructural code. You can petition your government. You can appeal a ban. But the system executing your exclusion isn't accountable to the channel you're speaking through. The forum exists. It just no longer governs.

VII. Upstream Design as the Enforcement Grid

The most consequential shift described in this section is not the rise of surveillance, automation, or programmable currency. It is the migration of enforcement into upstream design. Rules no longer emerge through visible negotiation or judicial review. They are pre-coded into the platforms we use, the payment systems we depend on, and the logistics layers we cannot bypass.

Upstream control, central to Big Tech architecture, the surveillance mesh, and emergency governance protocols, defines the structure of modern power: a system where noncompliance is not punished, but preemptively rendered impossible. The action is not blocked. It is never allowed to initialize.

VIII. Who This System Serves

The operating layer serves those for whom continuity, rather than public accountability, is the nonnegotiable variable. It protects financial institutions, national security contractors, central banks, and regulatory bodies whose legitimacy does not depend on electoral cycles, but on uninterrupted enforcement capacity. It serves global actors who have modeled out a future of permanent volatility, and have designed systems that will remain functional even if public trust collapses entirely.

As we will explore, these infrastructures are no longer contained within national borders. They are rapidly globalizing through interoperable CBDCs, cross-border digital identity schemes, and standardized enforcement APIs. What began as domestic infrastructure is becoming a planetary interface for managed eligibility.

This is not the shadow state. It is the substrate state. It's the default condition beneath governance, beneath law, beneath the last illusion that public life is still negotiated in public view.

Digital Identity as Enforcement Substrate

How Identification Systems Became Eligibility Systems

I. The Interface of Recognition

Identity has become an access point. Where analog systems once confirmed who you were, digital identity frameworks now determine what you are allowed to do. This shift is not cosmetic. It is functional. A paper credential proves existence. A digital credential grants permission. Every login, scan, or verification becomes a conditional access event. This is no longer a system of recognition. It is one of eligibility enforcement that is continuous, invisible, and real-time.

II. From Authentication to Access Control

Digital ID systems like India's Aadhaar, the EU's eIDAS framework, and the UN-backed ID2020 began as efficiency upgrades: faster verification, centralized records, reduced fraud. But over time, they undergo function creep (the gradual expansion of a system's purpose beyond its initial scope). In India, Aadhaar now gates access to subsidies, pensions, and school enrollment. In Estonia, digital ID is mandatory for voting, banking, and medical care. Eligibility is no longer a static status. It is recalculated at each checkpoint, based on system conformity. Governments expand these systems to streamline administration. Corporations leverage them to optimize behavioral data into profit. The result is the same: every act of verification becomes a moment of evaluation.

III. Interoperability as Global Governance

Although digital ID systems are deployed by national governments, they are increasingly standardized through international protocols. Interoperability, the ability of systems to share data across borders and platforms, is now a design feature, not a technical accident. Frameworks from ISO, the World Bank, and the World Economic Forum ensure alignment between ID, financial access, vaccination history, and geolocation. The World Bank's ID4D initiative defines digital ID as "foundational" for development. But when foundational becomes universal, exclusion becomes structural. A person without ID is functionally erased from most formal systems, as workarounds are limited, fragile, and often temporary. As we will see in the upcoming chapter on global harmonization, this standardization is not passive, it is governance by design.

IV. Conditional Inclusion and Silent Exile

Digital ID does not outlaw participation. It conditions it. In Nigeria, telecom access is now tied to the National Identification Number (NIN). In Canada, digital ID proposals link credentials to credit and law enforcement records. In both cases, a single credential governs mobility, finance, and communication. While partial compliance may allow temporary access, it reinforces dependency. Non-compliant users face escalating restrictions. Denial appears procedural: an expired login, a missing form, a failed match. It does not appear punitive. You are not rejected. You are offboarded.

V. The Merging of Identity and Behavior

When digital identity systems are fused with behavioral data such as purchase history, geolocation, and browser activity, they become tools of prediction, not just verification. China's national ID feeds directly into its social credit infrastructure, assigning scores that regulate housing, transportation, and education. In the West, Apple, Google, and Meta use similar ID layers to verify and monitor users. These systems don't declare compliance. They score it. Behavioral data feeds algorithms that assign risk levels, dynamically adjusting access to services like loans or travel based on predicted conformity. As we explored in the analysis of surveillance networks, this model of upstream formatting ensures that refusal is rare, not because dissent is banned, but because non-compliance is preemptively filtered out.

VI. Crisis-Activated Lockouts

Emergencies now activate credential regimes. The COVID-19 pandemic normalized this shift. Vaccine passports functioned as ad hoc digital IDs, used to permit or restrict access to transit, venues, and employment. Though framed as temporary, such measures established precedents. In China, the post-COVID health code system (originally a crisis response) has become a permanent eligibility layer. The EU's proposed Digital Identity Wallet embeds health records, travel data, and legal status into a single framework, suggesting a permanent model of dynamic access control based on crisis logic. During the 2022 Freedom Convoy protests, Canada froze bank accounts tied to flagged IDs. As shown in the chapter on financial enforcement, digital ID enables these lockouts to operate without judicial input. The result is not punishment. It is automated exclusion.

VII. Public-Private Credential Regimes

Credential systems are now infrastructural, not governmental. Mastercard's ID2020, Microsoft's decentralized ID protocols (which store identity across distributed nodes rather than a central authority), and Apple's biometric ID efforts represent a convergence. Corporate ID systems appear market-driven. They are framed as user-friendly, secure, efficient, but they align with state and supranational agendas through regulatory incentives and data-sharing agreements. Mastercard's ID2020 protocol, for example, complies with UN-backed standards that enforce eligibility requirements embedded into its architecture. These systems do not write law. They enforce rule sets. Terms of access are encoded. They are not voted on, nor debated. As we saw in the chapter on platform governance, power migrates to the pipe.

VIII. Who This System Serves

Digital identity systems serve institutions that benefit from conditional access at scale. Governments gain silent enforcement mechanisms. Corporations gain predictive consumer control. International bodies gain standardization without democratic friction. The ID is not a passport. It is a programmable gate. It can dim, suspend, or revoke access without ever signaling denial. Nothing is confiscated. Nothing is blocked. It is simply not granted. This is not a system of inclusion. It is a mechanism of filtration, one that requires no confrontation, only compliance.

Algorithmic Visibility and Digital Erasure

How Platforms Decide Who Gets Seen and Who Gets Forgotten

I. Speech Isn't Free If No One Hears It

Censorship today doesn't require a ban. It doesn't need a warning label or a takedown notice. All it takes is invisibility. If no one sees your words, you haven't been silenced, you've been erased. The platform still functions. You can still post. You can still speak. But you're trapped in an echo chamber where the lights are on and no one is listening.

II. The Feed Is a Filter, Not a Window

We treat the feed like a mirror of what's happening. It's not. It's a ranking system. A curated list. A behavioral prediction engine. What you see is mostly selected, not posted, and platforms typically serve engagement, not truth. You can't rebel against what you never knew existed.

III. Virality Is Manufactured

What goes viral is not what's important. It's what's promotable. Platforms elevate what keeps you engaged and that's usually anything that makes you angry, amused, scared, or validated. Substance is buried beneath performance. Quality loses to cadence. Accuracy loses to repetition. The system doesn't ask if it's true. It asks if it will hold attention.

Not everything algorithmically suppressed is controversial. Some posts never go viral not because they failed to resonate, but because they were never allowed to try. Early suppression before engagement data accumulates ensures that dissenting ideas never register as content trends. The system doesn't need to censor what it can pre-ignore. You're not silenced after success. You're erased before impact.

IV. Shadowbans and Quiet Repression

When content is manually removed, it becomes news. But when content is quietly suppressed, algorithmically downranked, removed from search, or shown only to a fraction of your audience, no one notices. Shadowbanning isn't hypothetical. X's 2023 "deboosting" leaks showed how critics of the platform were suppressed without notification (The Intercept). On X, users call this "posting to ghosts", an invisible punishment with no appeal.

V. Engagement as Obedience Test

The system rewards you for playing by its rules. Post often. Use the right tone. Avoid certain words. Be controversial, but not disruptive. Be emotional, but not off-brand. If you drift from the acceptable range, for example if your nuance threatens coherence or your critique targets advertisers, you will be deprioritized. Not punished. Just unseen.

VI. Content Moderation Without Accountability

We are told moderation is about safety. And sometimes it is. But moderation primarily prioritizes liability over safety, even as platforms tout tools like TikTok's 2024 child protection filters. Legal risk. Political optics. Investor pressure. The rules change constantly. Enforcement is inconsistent. And appeals go nowhere.

YouTube's 2024 demonetization of mental health content, citing vague "safety concerns," revealed that what matters most isn't protection. It's plausible deniability.

The algorithm doesn't just downrank. It distorts. Posts can be stripped of context through preview clipping, delayed display, or the removal of comment history. A nuanced argument becomes an out-of-context image. A correction never catches up to its viral misfire. What remains is an illusion of what was said. shaped by what the system lets linger. Visibility is granted, but understanding is sabotaged.

VII. The Algorithm Doesn't Forget Who You Are

Platform behavior is cumulative. Your history follows you. A wrong post, a flagged comment, a short burst of anger, or a week of inactivity all contribute to training the machine. And that training never resets, despite GDPR protections and opt-outs that promise deletion but rarely deliver in full. The algorithm, harvesting data like Cambridge Analytica did in 2018, builds your shadow self and feeds it back to you until your profile becomes your prison.

VIII. Attention as Currency, Silence as Debt

In a world where visibility is currency, silence becomes punishment. If you are not seen, you are not known. If you are not known, you cannot shape perception, defend yourself, or influence outcomes. You may still be speaking. But you're invisible. And that invisibility becomes your default state unless you learn to perform.

IX. Performance Over Truth

On most platforms, truth does not compete well. What wins is formatting, tone, timing, and familiarity. The post that mimics the system best will be seen the most. Not because it's right but because it looks like what the system wants. The reward is not accuracy. It's compatibility. This shift turns every user into a performer. To be seen, you must adapt by tweaking tone, formatting, volume, and pacing until you match the platform's expected cadence. Over time, this becomes second nature. Not out of fear, but out of hunger for reach. Self-censorship evolves into auto-formatting. The algorithm becomes less a gatekeeper than a script. You're still speaking but only in the voice it trained you to use.

X. Algorithmic Identity Enforcement

Once the platform believes it knows who you are, it stops listening. Your political leanings, your purchasing habits, your engagement patterns, these don't just shape what you see. They shape what you're allowed to say. TikTok's FYP reinforces political silos, nudging users back to type and limiting contradictory content (Wired, 2023). Step outside the frame, and the system assumes you're wrong.

XI. Disappearance by Design

Deplatforming doesn't always look like a ban. Sometimes it's just friction. Your links don't preview. Your images load slowly. Your content is labeled sensitive. Your reach drops suddenly. No explanation. No appeal. Just the slow erosion of presence. Not because you violated the rules but because you stopped fitting the model.

XII. Compliant Creators, Silenced Critics

Influencers who align with platform values are rewarded with reach. They say nothing controversial, criticize nothing structural, and model everything aspirational. Instagram's fitness influencers, like @FitFam, thrive by avoiding controversy. They sell positivity, aesthetics, and compliance in equal parts (Vox, 2024). Their success becomes proof that the system is fair. Meanwhile, critics, especially those who question the platforms themselves, fade. Not because they're wrong. But because they don't serve the machine.

XIII. The Illusion of Platform Neutrality

We still act like platforms are public squares. But they're not. They're curated cages. Privately owned, advertiser-funded, opaque by design. Their logic isn't civic. It's commercial. They don't show you what matters. They show you what performs. Platform logic echoes WEF's 2023 Meta partnership on "trustworthy feeds," a joint effort to algorithmically sanitize dissent in the name of digital hygiene. The rest isn't suppressed. It's forgotten.

XIV. What You Don't See Can't Go Viral

You cannot share what you never saw. You cannot defend what you never heard. The internet was supposed to democratize speech. But visibility is power, and power is not evenly distributed. You were never shown the full map. You were shown a lane. And told to scroll in their maze.

Military-Corporate Media After 9/11

How Security Narratives Became the Operating System of Public Perception

I. The Convergence Begins

After September 11, 2001, the United States entered a new phase of perception management. Intelligence agencies, defense contractors, and dominant media institutions increasingly adopted shared premises: that information was no longer neutral, and that narrative control was a strategic asset. While some outlets resisted, such as *The Nation* or *Democracy Now,* mainstream news and entertainment entities moved toward alignment with institutional power. This shift was not spontaneous. The Pentagon's 2003 *Information Operations Roadmap*, declassified in 2006, explicitly outlined strategies for shaping domestic perception, blurring the traditional divide between foreign psyops and domestic messaging. Psychological operations (military strategies designed to influence belief and behavior) quietly migrated inward.

II. Security as Content Filter

National security became the dominant filter for mass media content. Hollywood's longstanding relationship with the Department of Defense accelerated. Through script approvals, military consultants, and equipment loans, studios entered direct partnerships that linked narrative approval to logistical support. The result was not coercion but harmonization, driven by financial incentives and access agreements. Shows like *24* and films like

Zero Dark Thirty normalized torture, extrajudicial action, and surveillance as necessary tools in a perpetual threat environment. These portrayals, viewed by tens of millions, shaped public opinion. Pew Research in 2009 found a marked increase in American support for torture following exposure to such narratives. While framed as entertainment, the product was onboarding for a security worldview.

III. The Newscast as Theater of Legitimacy

Newsrooms followed a parallel track. Homeland Security briefings, advertiser demand for threat-driven content, and editorial self-selection gradually repurposed journalism as a system continuity layer. Slogans like "If you see something, say something" were not merely public safety messages. They were narrative reframers, teaching viewers to associate ambiguity with latent threat. Editorial hiring reinforced this shift. CNN, MSNBC, and Fox each began hiring former intelligence and military officials as on-air contributors, subtly embedding institutional alignment into everyday reporting. As explored in the chapter on continuity enforcement, this model did not seek to inform the public. It sought to stabilize them.

IV. Dissent as Instability Signal

Following the post-9/11 fusion of surveillance and domestic policing, protest was recast as volatility. Coverage of demonstrations, whether antiwar, anti-corporate, or anti-police, shifted from message to disruption: crowd size, conflict, threat potential. By 2020, this lens applied across ideological lines. Racial justice protests, COVID-era lockdown rallies, and anti-mandate convoys were all covered through the same template:

disruption equals danger. As described in the chapter on behavioral surveillance, this framing becomes data feeding into predictive risk models that flag non-compliant individuals for downstream exclusion from platforms, banking access, and reputation systems.

Social platforms didn't replace legacy media. They amplified its logic. Twitter and Facebook accelerated threat-lens framing by mirroring headlines through algorithmic virality. Video clips of clashes, hashtags linked to risk narratives, and moderation systems prioritizing "safety" over context all reinforced the same premise: visible dissent equals public disorder. This wasn't an organic response. It was formatting. Platforms, under pressure from intelligence partnerships and policy initiatives, quietly reshaped civic expression to align with continuity goals.

V. Information Operations Go Domestic

The legal boundary between government messaging and journalism collapsed under policy and practice. The 2013 Smith-Mundt Modernization Act lifted restrictions on U.S. government messaging campaigns targeting domestic audiences. Simultaneously, intelligence veterans began migrating into tech firms. Former CIA officer Dawn Meyerriecks joined Meta. Former NSA official Matt Olsen was hired by Uber. These individuals helped shape moderation policies informed by FBI task force protocols and counterinsurgency doctrine, which are military tactics to control threats by shaping information and isolating dissent, now adapted to platform environments. Twitter's coordinated suppression of COVID-19 vaccine debates, Facebook's removal of protest organizing pages, and the Hunter Biden laptop story are not isolated events. They are indicators of systemic alignment.

As institutions moved messaging online, a new class of soft propagandist emerged: the influencer-as-anchor. Ex-military YouTubers, verified TikTok health experts, and intelligence-adjacent podcasters filled the vacuum once held by newsrooms. These creators, often independently branded but institutionally adjacent, normalize official narratives through affective trust. The message is informal, but the impact is industrial. Viewers absorb state-adjacent positions through parasocial connection, not through critical inquiry.

VI. Pre-Legitimization and Manufactured Consensus

Narratives no longer trail reality. They preframe it. Media outlets, guided by intelligence leaks and PR firms, now deploy pre-legitimization: shaping public perception before full facts emerge. This ensures that public interpretation falls within accepted parameters from the outset. PR firms like Edelman coordinate with government agencies to preposition talking points. During the 2020 protests, coverage appeared within hours, echoing the same frames across CNN, MSNBC, and BBC. This is not conspiracy. It is convergence of formatting logic. The media system does not need orders. It operates from a shared template. As the upcoming chapter on cultural exports will show, these packages travel globally and standardize not just stories, but worldviews.

VII. Crisis as Normal Operating Conditions

The language of war has been grafted onto everyday governance. Domestic extremism, misinformation, health policy, and cybercrime are now addressed in national security terms. Threat levels have largely replaced journalistic neutrality in dominant media environments. While independent outlets persist like Substack, ProPublica, and independent podcasts, the institutional layer has absorbed the logic of continuity. The U.S. *National Strategy for Countering Domestic Terrorism* explicitly outlines media alignment goals. The UK's Prevent programme and Australia's cybersecurity statutes apply military rhetoric to local dissent. As the digital identity chapter showed, eligibility now extends beyond credentials. It includes belief conformity. Narrative becomes a precondition for access.

VIII. Who This System Serves

This system serves institutions that require legitimacy without direct public consent: defense contractors, intelligence agencies, and platform-media conglomerates that operate as infrastructure. Narrative gating, the restriction of visibility for stories that fall outside the dominant frame, ensures coherence across domains. While rare exceptions like *The Intercept* or *ProPublica* break through, their reach is often muted by algorithmic throttling or media exclusion. The approved story is amplified. Deviations are buried. Visibility itself becomes a reward for compliance. As we saw with digital identity systems, it is not about direct censorship. It is about conditional inclusion. The story continues uninterrupted. The nonconforming voice is never heard.

Cultural Exports as Global Alignment

How Entertainment Became a Delivery System for Soft Control

I. Image as Infrastructure

Culture travels faster than policy. In the post-9/11 era, global entertainment exports such as film, music, fashion, and social media have operated as soft governance (influencing behavior through cultural and ideological means rather than direct policy). Hollywood blockbusters, K-Pop idols, and algorithmically promoted influencers do more than entertain. They instruct. Ideological compliance is taught not by decree, but through aesthetic habituation, through repeated exposure to curated images, behaviors, and narratives that appear natural. What looks like art often functions as policy in disguise.

II. Hollywood as Behavioral Template

Hollywood has always been a projection system that attempts framing American values as universal. After 2001, its alignment with national security interests accelerated. Pentagon, CIA, and FBI partnerships shaped scripts, supplied equipment, and approved narratives. While films like *The Hurt Locker*, *V for Vendetta*, or *Avatar* critique militarism and corporate power, dominant Hollywood blockbusters, especially those backed by Pentagon resources, frame resistance as irrational and power as efficient. As explored in the chapter on media control, this alignment is enforced not through censorship, but through conditional access: studios must comply to receive assets. *Zero*

Dark Thirty, backed by Pentagon consultants, promoted the efficacy of torture, coinciding with a Gallup poll spike in public support for harsh interrogation methods. Studios often claim to follow market demand, but security-aligned content is made profitable through subsidies, resource access, and media amplification.

III. K-Pop, Poptimism, and Cosmetic Obedience

South Korea's K-Pop industry, which is subsidized, regulated, and tightly curated, functions as a soft power export model. Behind its global appeal lies behavioral discipline: media training, speech restrictions, and adherence to state norms. Though presented as apolitical, the government has imposed messaging constraints on artists, including BTS in 2018 during diplomatic tensions. The global fan experience isn't just musical. It is aspirational. Conformity is presented as empowerment. Fans internalize behavioral cues: brand alignment, performative harmony, and algorithmic participation. As the chapter on digital identity showed, this mirrors eligibility systems where expression is permitted only within preapproved bounds.

IV. The Algorithm as Moral Editor

Streaming platforms and social media do not merely host content, they rank, recommend, and suppress based on internal risk models. Netflix originals increasingly center identity-affirming, politically inert narratives. But this is not unique. YouTube's 2021 deboosting of anti-vaccine channels, and Spotify's removal of politically sensitive content, show how platforms filter ambiguity and reward compliance. While platforms like pre-2022 X occasionally amplified controversial content, dominant streaming and social systems prioritize alignment with advertiser safety and institutional norms. Algorithms are trained on risk markers such as language, tone, and subject matter, and downrank content that deviates from platform priorities. User choice persists, but only within a pre-sorted catalog.

V. Influencers as Compliance Vectors

Influencer culture breaks compliance into digestible, self-managed parts. Each influencer becomes a node in a distributed network of ideological enforcement, framing political issues through personal branding. Trust is central. Audiences see these figures as peers, not authorities. But the content is strategically depoliticized. Climate change becomes a question of product choice. Civil unrest becomes a post about self-care. This is cause marketing (the promotion of social issues through consumer behavior). Algorithms reward such framing, ensuring visibility for messages that convert political concern into corporate-compatible expression. As the perception management chapter demonstrated, this is not the absence of politics. It is its replacement.

VI. Censorship Without the Word

Exportable culture is not censored in the traditional sense. It is edited pre-distribution. Scripts are adjusted to avoid offending censors in China, the Gulf states, or multinational sponsors. Music videos are sanitized for geopolitical neutrality. Game releases are delayed to avoid controversy. While niche content occasionally reaches audiences through independent platforms, and rare controversies like *Cuties* spark backlash, mainstream exports are pre-smoothed to minimize dissonance. Dissonant stories are quietly buried. Audiences encounter no denial, only a narrowed menu. As with digital ID and CBDC systems, exclusion is not announced. It is silently applied.

VII. Globalization as Alignment Layer

What circulates globally is not raw culture. It is pre-validated content formatted for interoperability. Streaming platforms localize language but not logic. Korean dramas, American thrillers, and European documentaries pass through the same ideological gatekeepers. Even where aesthetic diversity is permitted, structural assumptions remain intact: institutional legitimacy, safe rebellion, individualized morality. The earlier chapter on military-media convergence showed how domestic narratives were harmonized. Here, the same formatting is exported. As the next chapter will explore, supranational institutions like the WEF use these systems not as entertainment, but as alignment tools to standardize perception at scale.

VIII. Who This System Serves

This export structure serves governments seeking soft legitimacy, corporations seeking market stability, and global governance frameworks seeking behavioral standardization. The viewer is not denied content. They are surrounded by it. But every rebellion is safe. Every identity is pre-cleared. Culture becomes spectacle without risk. The algorithm keeps streaming. The feed keeps refreshing. And the user, surrounded by infinite variation, forgets that every choice was curated before they arrived.

Climate Narratives and Sustainability as Soft Governance

How Environmental Rhetoric Became an Enforcement Interface

I. The Language of Urgency

Climate change is real. Its effects are material. But the way its urgency has been translated into governance language reveals a parallel agenda: behavioral formatting. Climate narratives have migrated from ecological concern to infrastructural control. They now underpin economic scoring systems, digital credentials, and access frameworks. What began as scientific warning has become soft governance, shaping behavior through cultural, economic, or ideological tools rather than direct laws. Compliance replaces consensus. The threat is planetary, so participation becomes conditional.

II. From Consensus to Compliance

While grassroots movements like Fridays for Future and Extinction Rebellion persist, the dominant climate narrative is increasingly shaped by multilateral institutions, regulatory alliances, and corporate partnerships. Institutions such as the World Economic Forum, the UN Environment Programme, and the International Sustainability Standards Board steer climate messaging through ESG metrics, investment gatekeeping, and curated media campaigns. WEF-funded partnerships, like Bloomberg's 2021 net-zero media initiative, promote narrative alignment by tying funding to ESG-compliant content. While actions like renewable energy adoption reflect ecological priorities, institutional frameworks prioritize political standardization over bottom-up environmental solutions. What gets implemented is not just science. It is science curated into strategy.

The appearance of global consensus on climate strategy is often maintained by excluding dissenting ecological models rather than debating them. Degrowth, localized resilience, and indigenous stewardship frameworks receive minimal coverage in ESG-aligned media, despite academic legitimacy. Their omission is not accidental, it's structural. Multilateral bodies, funded by growth-dependent economies, prioritize scalable solutions that preserve investment flows. Climate messaging becomes not a contest of ideas, but a filtering mechanism. The story remains uniform because alternatives are never introduced.

III. ESG as a Behavioral Filter

ESG scoring (a system evaluating companies and individuals on environmental impact, social policies, and governance practices) began as a corporate accountability mechanism. It now operates as a behavioral filter. ESG criteria increasingly determine access to loans, partnerships, and legitimacy and not only for companies, but for individuals. Banks like HSBC, through 2023 ESG-linked lending programs, have begun assessing borrowers' carbon footprints using transaction data. A 2024 ECB report found that 15% of European banks now incorporate such filters. While ESG appears to promote accountability, its individual applications prioritize behavioral control over emissions reduction. As seen in the chapter on digital identity, noncompliance does not trigger punishment. It triggers invisibility. You are not penalized. You are disqualified.

IV. The Green Wallet Prototype

Green wallets, which fuse environmental tracking with digital payments, are moving from concept to infrastructure. Mastercard's 2021 carbon calculator app, developed with Doconomy, lets users set voluntary emissions limits. But the infrastructure behind it is more expansive. Mastercard's 2023 API partnerships with central banks integrate carbon thresholds into payment protocols. The ECB's 2023 digital euro pilot tested mandatory carbon limits for select users, enforcing real-time purchase restrictions based on emissions. Though marketed as empowering, these wallets enable enforcement by embedding behavioral constraints into financial rails. The shift from voluntary to mandatory doesn't require new legislation, only regulatory alignment and a firmware update.

Many climate apps now incorporate gamification like scores, badges, and weekly streaks to encourage "eco-friendly" behavior. While presented as motivational, this design masks compliance as play. Users are trained to self-regulate via psychological triggers, reinforcing system-defined norms. This mirrors social credit logics discussed in earlier chapters: behavior becomes performance, and reward replaces freedom. You aren't forced to change. You're nudged until you forget it was ever optional.

V. The Climate Passport Concept

Carbon tracking (using apps or digital tools to monitor and limit personal or corporate carbon emissions) is already active in consumer platforms. Digital IDs authenticate identity.

Programmable wallets enforce transaction rules. The "climate passport," which conditions access to flights, food, or energy on emissions history, is no longer speculative. A 2023 WEF white paper outlined a framework for interoperable carbon IDs. Singapore's 2023 carbon credit scheme piloted individual emissions budgets for mobility and lifestyle choices. While pilots like these show metering is feasible, global scalability will depend on unified ID and payment systems. As with the digital identity chapter, these systems don't criminalize behavior. They gate it. Exceed your limit, and the option disappears.

Carbon offsets, once framed as market-based sustainability tools, now function as economic enclosures. High-income individuals and corporations can purchase exemptions, while low-income users face hard caps. The system mirrors elite continuity programs discussed in previous chapters: those with resources navigate around restrictions, while compliance is enforced below. Offsets don't neutralize emissions, they neutralize accountability. What began as environmental compensation becomes an access toll, paid by those who can afford movement inside a gated sustainability regime.

VI. Crisis Framing as Policy Pipeline

The climate emergency is framed not as an ecological event but as a permanent justification layer, mirroring post-9/11 and pandemic-era policy models. Crisis becomes the new interface for infrastructure rollout. The EU's Green Deal, fast-tracked in 2020 without referenda, embedded long-term mandates through emergency clauses. Those clauses were extended via 2024 regulatory updates, enabling annual climate targets without public consultation. As explored in the chapter on media alignment, climate threat language is formatted by partnerships that pre-legitimize policy before debate can occur. What begins as urgency becomes continuity. The infrastructure remains, long after the emergency fades.

VII. Who Decides What Counts as Sustainable

Sustainability is now defined by global frameworks and private standards boards. ISO guidelines, WEF proposals, and ESG ratings determine which products, services, and behaviors count. These decisions shape access across sectors. Farmers are told which inputs qualify for climate funds. Travelers are told which offset programs are valid. Developers are told which projects meet green thresholds. As noted in the chapter on cultural exports, this system doesn't demand uniformity. It demands interoperable obedience, with behavior shaped to align with global systems through compatible rules and standards. Sustainability becomes a compatibility check; if your actions do not conform, your access is denied.

VIII. Who This System Serves

Climate based governance serves governments seeking control without resistance, corporations seeking subsidy and insulation, and supranational actors seeking influence without consent. You are not told to stop consuming. You are redirected toward approved goods, routes, and platforms. The system calls it empowerment. The interface says sustainability. But what's enforced is eligibility: not through bans, but through design. As the next section will explore, these systems are converging, not as parallel reforms, but as a unified control grid administered above the level of democracy.

Trade Law Harmonization as Regulatory Capture

How Treaties and Technical Bodies Override National Policy

I. The Hidden Treaties

Modern trade law is no longer confined to tariffs and customs duties. It has become a vehicle for enforcing global compliance through binding policy frameworks. Agreements like the Trans-Pacific Partnership (TPP), the United States–Mexico–Canada Agreement (USMCA), and protocols from the World Trade Organization (WTO) now dictate rules not just on commerce, but also on labor law, environmental regulation, intellectual property, data access, and digital services. While these treaties can technically be renegotiated or exited, as the United States did with the original TPP in 2017, their complexity, embedded institutional commitments, and corporate backing make meaningful change through a single election nearly impossible.

Proponents argue these agreements foster growth. However, as Mexico's 2020 agricultural concessions under the USMCA illustrate, that growth often comes with hidden costs: forced deregulation, market flooding, and structural disadvantage for local producers. The appearance of economic prosperity masks the deeper reality that trade law functions as an enforcement surface where compliance is not negotiated but pre-written.

II. Regulatory Capture by Design

Regulatory harmonization, which refers to aligning national laws with global standards to facilitate trade, is often framed as a neutral efficiency measure. In reality, it enables capture. These treaties are rarely negotiated in public. Industry lobbyists, not elected officials, frequently shape the agenda. During the TPP negotiations, more than 500 corporate advisors had access to the draft texts, including representatives from Pfizer, Monsanto, and the Motion Picture Association of America. In contrast, most lawmakers and the general public were locked out of the process.

Corporate advisors shaped diluted environmental and labor standards by embedding industry-friendly language directly into the drafts, as revealed by the 2015 Wikileaks disclosures. Data localization laws, which require a nation's data to be stored within its borders, were weakened or preemptively prohibited in favor of unrestricted cloud service growth. The result is regulatory uniformity that reflects corporate priorities. Once embedded in a treaty, these preferences are enforced across jurisdictions, and deviation becomes a breach of contract rather than an act of national self-determination.

This structure formats legal systems in the same way curated cultural narratives format perception. What used to be a domestic policy debate is now an obligation inherited from a supranational document.

III. Intellectual Property as a Control Surface

The intellectual property regime, largely managed by the World Intellectual Property Organization (WIPO), has shifted from protecting creators to maintaining monopolies. Copyright, patent, and trademark protections have steadily expanded in both scope and duration. These provisions are embedded in trade treaties and enforced through legal mechanisms, including WTO sanctions and retaliatory tariffs.

When India attempted to issue compulsory licenses for generic versions of life-saving drugs, U.S. pharmaceutical firms lobbied to bring the case to the WTO. In 2018, the resulting pressure forced India to suspend several license programs. Brazil faced similar backlash for its efforts to bypass proprietary agricultural technologies. Although WIPO frames itself as a neutral body supporting innovation, its enforcement structure overwhelmingly defends established firms.

This is not a symbolic regime. It has material impact. As discussed in the digital identity chapter, access is now determined through credentialing. In intellectual property, this logic applies to medicine, research tools, and even digital content. Without the proper license, there is no access.

IV. ICANN and the Privatization of the Internet

The internet's backbone is now privately administered. ICANN, the Internet Corporation for Assigned Names and Numbers, governs domain name systems, root server hierarchies, and technical standards for website functionality. Although ICANN presents itself as a neutral administrative entity, it exercises real control over digital access.

In 2020, ICANN suspended .org domain registrations for several registrars that failed to meet internal security standards, citing "stability risks." In 2021, domain names linked to decentralized platforms were denied approval. And in 2022, domains tied to sanctioned Russian and Iranian institutions were disabled without appeal. ICANN does not ban content. It removes access to the address. The website might still exist, but no one can find it.

While defenders of ICANN argue that it is a technical body, its decisions are deeply political in effect. They shape who can be found online, under what name, and on whose terms. As noted in the digital identity chapter, visibility has become conditional. ICANN exemplifies this by quietly determining who gets to participate in the digital public square.

Many trade agreements now require technological "interoperability," a term that functionally mandates the use of specific global platforms. WTO and USMCA provisions require access for foreign digital service providers under "non-discriminatory treatment" clauses. This often compels governments to integrate platforms like Google, Amazon, and Meta into public-facing systems, even when domestic alternatives exist. What appears as openness is actually obligation. National agencies become tenants in privately owned infrastructure that they are legally bound to rent.

V. Harmonization as Eligibility Gatekeeping

Harmonization does not feel like coercion. It presents itself as a condition of entry. Participation in global trade networks, international finance, and digital infrastructure often depends on meeting harmonized standards related to cybersecurity, intellectual property, ESG metrics, and data governance. Countries that fall short may not be penalized directly. Instead, they are excluded from critical systems.

Venezuela's 2019 exclusion from the SWIFT financial messaging network was justified through regulatory noncompliance. At the same time, China has maintained selective adherence to WTO rules while retaining access to global markets. This inconsistency reveals how harmonization operates asymmetrically. Weak states are disciplined. Strong ones negotiate exceptions.

Trade law uses the same framing found in media and military narratives. Noncompliance is positioned as economic suicide. Divergence is rebranded as instability. What begins as a treaty becomes an eligibility framework, where access to capital, platforms, and legitimacy depends on how well a country conforms to upstream rules.

Harmonization is also enforced through secondary financial mechanisms like insurance underwriting and country risk ratings. A nation that refuses to comply with trade-aligned standards may find itself downgraded by firms like Moody's or denied coverage by global insurers. These mechanisms don't legislate behavior, they price it. The cost of divergence becomes prohibitive, not through sanctions, but through invisible friction: higher interest rates, investor pullouts, and collapsed underwriting for critical infrastructure. Governance becomes actuarial. The penalty is not declared. It is invoiced.

VI. The Displacement of Sovereignty

Harmonization does not eliminate sovereignty. It relocates its power center. Policymakers may propose legislation on renewable energy, labor protections, or digital regulation. However, if those policies conflict with harmonized trade rules, they become functionally inert. Procedural blockades, defined as legal or economic restrictions built into trade agreements, prevent implementation.

India's clean energy subsidies were blocked by a 2020 WTO ruling. Hungary's attempt to re-nationalize utility pricing was overridden by EU competition law. Poland's judicial reforms were constrained through market access threats. These governments still exist, but their freedom to act is capped by agreements signed decades prior.

As described in the chapter on climate narratives, even well-intentioned reforms related to sustainability or local control are limited by ESG and emissions frameworks embedded into trade pacts. The domestic policymaker is left with only one viable option: make changes that do not disrupt the external frame.

VII. The Unaccountable Layer

The enforcement layer behind trade harmonization, composed of WIPO boards, WTO panels, and ICANN committees, operates without direct democratic input. These institutions write, interpret, and enforce rules that govern the global flow of goods, services, information, and ideas. There is no electorate, no recall, and no public vote.

WIPO redefines what counts as protected expression. WTO panels overturn local subsidies. ICANN manages visibility itself. When a tribunal issues a ruling or an infrastructure body applies a sanction, the affected public has no formal mechanism for appeal. As outlined in the digital identity chapter, eligibility is not about inclusion. It is about access control. Once a system deems you noncompliant, your participation is no longer subject to debate.

Supporters of these institutions may insist that they serve as neutral arbiters. But their rulings consistently align with the interests of the largest stakeholders. As discussed in the chapter on cultural exports, what is enforced is not uniformity. It is compatibility with the system.

VIII. Who This System Serves

Trade harmonization benefits those who prioritize policy stability over public participation. Corporations gain access to global markets with consistent legal protections. Supranational institutions gain jurisdiction over issues previously reserved for national governments. Compliant states gain access to financing, platforms, and favorable trade terms.

What is lost in this process is the ability to act outside the harmonized frame. A country can hold elections, pass laws, and express local values. However, if those laws contradict upstream rules, they are rendered ineffective. Sovereignty exists in name but not in function.

As with digital ID frameworks, trade law has become a credentialing layer. As seen in the media infrastructure chapter, narrative discipline frames alternatives as dangerous or chaotic. And as the chapter on climate sustainability showed, even ecological reform is filtered through compatibility assessments.

The next chapter will examine how these systems, including legal, digital, narrative, and financial frameworks, are being combined into a global operating grid. This grid does not need permission to run. It requires only that you meet the entry requirements.

The Operating Layer

How Participation Became Decorative in a Fully Harmonized World

I. The End of Governance as We Knew It

The architecture of governance has shifted. What once relied on law, representation, and debate now operates through a layered mesh of elite coordination, infrastructural enforcement, and narrative containment. Traditional democratic forms like elections, public comment, and protest still persist. But they no longer shape the core operating logic of global power. Consent remains visible. It no longer remains decisive.

At the heart of this transformation is a migration of rule. Decisions are no longer made through deliberative politics. They are encoded into platforms, frameworks, and eligibility systems that filter participation through compatibility with upstream standards. These include ESG metrics, ISO technical protocols, WTO compliance audits, digital identity layers, and trade harmonization treaties. What counts is not what you vote for, but whether you conform.

II. Participation as Ritual, Not Power

Participation is still welcomed. Portals, dashboards, and surveys offer a sense of involvement. But their function has inverted. They now serve to absorb feedback, not to adjust policy. European climate consultations, U.S. agency comment systems, and global stakeholder reports all exhibit the same pattern: they record dissent while preserving predetermined outcomes. Input is routed. It is not implemented.

Even referenda and electoral wins yield conditional results. Switzerland's 2021 climate vote was overridden by EU-aligned policy constraints. Brexit triggered years of compliance renegotiations that reaffirmed many of the frameworks it sought to escape. In each case, the form of consent remained, but the field of consequence had been moved upstream.

III. Soft Consensus and the Displacement of Law

What replaced deliberation is soft consensus, an informal alignment of institutions that operate above direct accountability. The World Economic Forum, IMF, ISO, ICANN, WIPO, and global consultancy networks produce white papers, memoranda, and scorecard systems that are then implemented not by governments, but by banks, tech firms, regulatory boards, and app stores.

These frameworks are not legally binding. They do not need to be. They operate by setting thresholds for access. Institutions, individuals, and even governments must conform to these standards to maintain funding, visibility, or operational viability. This is enforcement without a mandate. Alignment becomes the cost of participation.

IV. Infrastructure as Enforcement

Constraint-by-design is now the dominant mode of control. Rather than using laws to prohibit behavior, modern systems embed compliance into technical infrastructure. If your app does not align with Apple's evolving data policies, it is delisted. If your comment triggers a platform risk filter, it is suppressed. If your emissions exceed ESG limits, your financial product is disabled. These outcomes are not framed as punishments. They are explained as protocol.

This dynamic extends to nations. Venezuela's removal from SWIFT, India's WTO loss over solar subsidies, and Iran's exclusion from trade infrastructure were not labeled as sanctions. They were procedural responses to non-compliance. These are not legal punishments. They are failures to meet inherited conditions. No appeals exist.

The aesthetics of participation mask its absence. Interfaces are optimized for usability, not transparency. Button placement, notification timing, and default settings are engineered to generate compliance without resistance. A form labeled "agree and continue" appears in every onboarding screen. The rules it enforces are already active before you click. You aren't coerced. You're streamlined. Governance happens through UX.

V. Eligibility as the New Citizenship

Access to participation now hinges on eligibility. This eligibility is determined by upstream frameworks, algorithmic gatekeeping, and compatibility with soft standards. You do not vote on content moderation rules. You adapt your behavior to stay visible. You do not choose what scorecard determines ESG compliance. You meet its terms to receive credit. Citizenship has become conditional. Rights have become transactional.

Eligibility determines access to platforms, banking, mobility, education, and speech. It is enforced through ID systems, financial APIs, content filters, and social scoring layers. Those who deviate are not prosecuted. They are ignored, deprioritized, or quietly disconnected. A post never loads. A payment fails. A loan application is declined. Exclusion happens without announcement. It is procedural, not personal.

VI. Decentralized Harmonization

This system is not centrally planned. It is harmonized. Compliance frameworks align through treaties, platforms, and code. Each node enforces its part, including Apple, Mastercard, Meta, UNDP, ICANN, and ISO, without full knowledge of the whole. Yet the effect is systemic. A flagged identity cascades. Financial access, social visibility, and physical movement all degrade in sync.

Each domain, including media, finance, mobility, and governance, feeds data into the next. A flagged phrase can affect search visibility. A search flag can affect platform standing. Platform standing can affect payment access. Payment access can affect state services. This is not conspiracy. It is interoperability.

These systems also shape outcomes by controlling time. Platform updates, treaty ratifications, and standards rollouts often occur with little notice, leaving users and even governments scrambling to adapt. The timing is not accidental. It is strategic. Surprise becomes structure. With no advance warning, compliance becomes the only viable path. Public response isn't suppressed—it is outpaced. Resistance lags. Implementation leads.

VII. A System Without a Return Address

Because no single actor controls this system, no one can be held responsible. A platform blames a standard. A standard cites a treaty. A treaty references environmental benchmarks. Each institution points upward or outward. The result is enforcement without authorship. Disconnection has no door to knock on.

This is what gives the system its durability. It cannot be repealed. It cannot be electorally overturned. It does not depend on mass belief. It functions through default protocols and alignment conditions. It is not imposed by fiat. It is sustained by interoperability.

VIII. What Replaces Consent

Consent has not vanished. It has been recontextualized. It now serves as an interface for managing perception, not power. You are invited to participate, provided your participation fits the form. Protest is permitted, but only in zones. Speech is allowed, but only within terms. Dissent is acknowledged, but only as metadata.

The system does not need your belief. It needs your data. It does not require your trust. It requires your compatibility. Those who align are granted access, resources, and amplification. Those who do not are not criminalized. They are rendered irrelevant.

This is the operating layer: a world in which rule is no longer negotiated, but inherited. Where legitimacy is not derived from the public, but from compliance with upstream protocols. Where citizenship is not a guarantee, but a credential. Where dissent is not punished, but preemptively routed into forms that cannot change outcomes.

You are free to participate. But only within a system that no longer needs your permission to function.

Pushing Back: What This Book Gets Wrong—and Why It Still Matters

This chapter is not a retraction. It is a reckoning.

By now, you have read a book that is openly biased. That bias was not an accident. It was the mechanism. The goal was to reveal a pattern of convergence in how institutions that appear independent, even benevolent, align in practice to script behavior, limit dissent, and mask coercion as consent.

But a pattern is not a proof. A polemic is not a peer review. And a voice raised in warning can still miss the mark.

This chapter exists to face those misses head-on. It is here to name the ways this book overstepped, oversimplified, or overstated. Not to weaken the argument, but to strengthen the reader's trust in its construction. What follows is a critical audit of this book's weakest points, framed not as a concession, but as a clarifier.

I. Slippery Slope Thinking

This book often draws lines between familiar behaviors and dystopian outcomes. It suggests that subscribing to services leads to dependency, that accepting personalization leads to performance, and that routine participation rituals render consent meaningless.

These are not hard predictions. They are illustrations of structural logic.

The argument is not that every small convenience leads to total control. It is that the systems are designed to reduce friction in ways that steer behavior. The book uses trajectory as a rhetorical device. When it says "this leads to that," it means this is how alignment functions when left unchecked.

If this book fails, it fails by not always labeling its projections clearly. In future editions or in discussion, it should clarify: these are not inevitabilities. These are emerging patterns, made more likely by their scale and design, not by any master plan.

II. Strawman Framing

Some of the institutions criticized here, such as schools, tech platforms, and NGOs, are portrayed as singular in motive. This is not true, and it was never meant to be.

Schools sometimes foster critical thinking. Tech platforms sometimes empower connection. NGOs sometimes fight power rather than serve it. These exceptions are real.

But exceptions are not the norm. And this book is about the norm.

The framing is aggressive because the quiet middle has been too patient. When people mistake polite bureaucracy for neutral structure, they fail to see how systems reinforce each other. The book names the most extreme tendencies not to ignore nuance, but to force it into the conversation. Still, in places, the caricatures come too easily. Future work should include more direct engagement with institutions that diverge from the pattern.

III. False Dichotomies

In many chapters, the reader is presented with a choice: participate and be controlled, or opt out and be punished. That binary is false. Many people navigate systems creatively. They use debt strategically. They manage notifications. They subscribe on their terms. They resist without exile.

The truth is: this book is written for those who feel the middle path slipping away. The dichotomies were not built for logic, they were built for empathy. To name the experience of people who try to "work the system" and find the system working them back.

That said, in several places the framing could have been widened. Readers should be reminded that middle paths still exist, and they deserve protection. The more polarized the structure becomes, the more valuable nuance becomes.

IV. Overgeneralization and Confirmation Bias

This book selects extreme examples. It amplifies system failures. It focuses on collapse, not compromise.

That was necessary for impact. But it risks mistaking the sharpest edge for the whole blade.

There are resilient school models. There are subscription services that benefit users. There are wellness programs that heal rather than shame. These truths are not ignored maliciously, but they are underrepresented. That weakens the book's credibility among readers who live in those exceptions.

The future version of this argument must be stronger. Not softer. Stronger. That means confronting what doesn't fit the pattern and explaining why it still matters.

V. Appeal to Emotion

This book uses metaphors like "behavioral leash," "structured surrender," "decorative participation." These are not measured phrases. They are designed to provoke, to trigger a reader's latent recognition.

But that strategy has a cost. Emotional framing can obscure empirical grounding. It can cause readers to feel manipulated even when the content is true.

In a world shaped by ad copy, press releases, and institutional gaslighting, emotion is sometimes the only honest response. But the next version of this critique should pair every moment of outrage with something harder than outrage—data, documentation, and lived examples.

This chapter is the beginning of that work.

VI. Post Hoc Reasoning

This book occasionally implies causation where only correlation exists. It observes a convergence of language, incentives, and outcomes across institutions, and then suggests that this alignment proves intent.

It does not.

Credit scores correlate with behavioral control, but they were born of actuarial math. Digital identity systems enable exclusion, but they were built for access. Surveillance programs suppress dissent, but they often began as crime prevention or public safety tools.

This book leans on proximity and repetition to imply design. That technique reveals structural coherence, but it cannot stand in for direct proof. Where it fails, it fails by implying that what happens together must have been planned together.

This chapter exists, in part, to name that failure. Patterns matter. But pattern recognition is not the same as conspiracy detection. This book is about how systems align, not who holds the master key.

VII. Ad Hominem by Implication

In several chapters, especially on debt, wellness, and platform participation, the book implies that people who comply are naive or complicit. That framing is a mistake.

Most people participate in coercive systems out of necessity, not ignorance. They are navigating the best choices available under constraint. They are optimizing survival, not endorsing control.

The language of "celebration," "self-curation," and "unwitting performance" sometimes erases this truth. It treats human beings as unaware, when most are simply exhausted.

To everyone reading who is still inside these systems. Everyone who uses credit, who works a platform, who posts gratitude to survive a job. That is not failure. That is adaptation. You are not the problem.

The problem is that adaptation has become the price of inclusion. And that price is rising.

VIII. Neglect of Agency

There are people resisting. There are people opting out. There are people building alternatives. This book did not say enough about them.

You'll find passing references to open-source software, homeschooling, and cooperative banking but they are not given the weight they deserve. That is a flaw in emphasis, not belief.

This book believes resistance matters. It also believes resistance is inefficient by design. The point was never that you *can't* say no.

The point is that saying no will cost you.

Still, by underplaying resistance, the book risks sounding like doom. Worse, it risks disrespecting those who fight.

That was not the intent. And this chapter is here to name the difference between being *trapped* and being *tired*.

People are not trapped. They are tired. They are punished for resisting. And they are punished so reliably that most eventually stop trying.

That does not mean the fence is fake. It means it is better hidden.

IX. Speculation on Intent

One of the most dangerous shortcuts in any critical work is assuming design where there may only be drift. This book sometimes crosses that line.

It hints that surveillance is coordinated, that personalization is psychological conditioning, that ESG frameworks are scripted to enforce global compliance. These are plausible interpretations, but they are not proven facts.

The more accurate claim is that these systems *align*. They reinforce each other. They adapt to similar pressures. They serve similar masters. That does not mean they were all built by the same hand.

Speculation is allowed in a polemic. It is a tool. But speculation should never wear the mask of certainty.

This chapter exists to remove that mask. If you ever felt that this book overstated the case, you were probably right. It overstates to make the pattern visible. Not because the truth needed help, but because the noise made it hard to hear.

X. No Call to Action

This book diagnoses. It dissects. It exposes. But it does not prescribe.

That absence is deliberate. This is not a how-to manual. It is a pattern interruption. It is the shout that comes *before* the plan. But that does not mean it should have stayed silent on solutions.

If this book leaves you angry, good. If it leaves you demoralized, that is a failure.

You deserve to know that people are building new tools. Local currencies. Food co-ops. Cooperative media. Encryption projects. Decentralized infrastructure. It's all happening. It's just not happening at scale.

The point of this book is not to offer a solution. It is to clear the fog. Because before you can fight, you have to see.

And now you've seen it.

XI. What the Tradeoff Bought

This book makes tradeoffs. It sacrifices balance for force. It prioritizes pattern over proof. It chooses polemic over polish. That was not an oversight. It was the cost of being heard.

There are more precise books than this one. There are more neutral books. There are better sourced, peer-reviewed, and academically restrained books. Some of them sit unread in open tabs and footnotes. Others, like the work of ProPublica, the Brookings Institution, or Amnesty International, do critical work in full daylight. They are not this book's enemy. They are its allies.

But this book was never meant to be one of them. It was not designed to explain. It was built to break the trance.

If some of the language here feels exaggerated, it often is. If some patterns seem stretched, they often are. But they are stretched for a reason. The systems being described do not announce themselves. They do not hide, either. They normalize. They harmonize. They repeat until even critics forget where the edges are.

Polemic is not the only way to see that. But for many readers, it may be the only way to feel it.

Still, polemic alone is not enough. It must be paired with evidence. With counterexamples. With resistance.

So here is what this book did not say loudly enough:

- Aadhaar helped over a billion people access public services. It also excluded many through mandatory linkage.
- ESG frameworks have incentivized some emissions reductions. They have also created new levers of behavioral sorting.
- Algorithms have surfaced marginalized voices and suppressed dissent, often at the same time.
- The problem is not always the system. It is what the system quietly becomes under pressure.

And here is what resistance looks like in practice:

- The **Tor Project** builds tools for anonymity.
- **Mastodon** offers a decentralized alternative to corporate

social media.

- **Signal** encrypts messages for activists, journalists, and everyday users.
- **Mondragon** demonstrates how large-scale worker-owned cooperatives can function in a global market.
- Food co-ops, zine libraries, mutual aid groups, and open-source developers build small autonomy daily, without permission.

If you are still participating in systems this book criticizes, you are not the problem. Adaptation is not complicity. Survival is not surrender.

But if this book did its job, you will not see those systems the same way again.

Polemic is a blunt tool. It is not precise. It is not gentle. It is not the last word.

It is the alarm clock.

Now that you are awake, the next step is yours.

Sources

Apple Inc. (n.d.). *Human Interface Guidelines*. Retrieved from https://developer.apple.com/design/human-interface-guidelines/

Bloomberg. (2024). BlackRock's ESG dashboard adds sentiment data from employee review platforms and social media.

Brookings Institution (2023). *What Went Wrong with Federal Student Loans?* Adam Looney & Constantine Yannelis. Brookings Institution, September 17, 2024.

Calcabrini, A., & Hamill, J. (2022, June 9). *Sustainability Communications Need to Get Real*. Ogilvy. Retrieved from https://www.ogilvy.com/ideas/sustainability-communications-need-get-real

Centers for Disease Control and Prevention (CDC, 2023). Discrimination in medical diagnostics.

Drake, C., Roehrs, T., Shambroom, J., & Roth, T. (2013). *Caffeine effects on sleep taken 0, 3, or 6 hours before going to bed. Journal of Clinical Sleep Medicine*, 9(11), 1195–1200.

Dunbar, R. I. M. (1992). *Neocortex size as a constraint on group size in primates. Journal of Human Evolution*, 22(6), 469–493.

ECB Digital Euro (2023). Tested programmable spending tied to emissions thresholds.

Edelman (2020–2024). PR firm cited for prepositioning talking points and coordinating crisis media narratives.

Eisenberger, N. I., & Lieberman, M. D. (2004). *Why it hurts to be left out: The neurocognitive overlap between physical and social pain. Trends in Cognitive Sciences*, 8(7), 294–300.

European Union Green Deal (2020, 2024). Fast-tracked with no public referendum; extended via 2024 regulatory updates.

Gartner. (2024). Over 40% of large employers use biometric productivity tools for behavioral evaluation.

ICANN (2020–2022). Suspended domain names tied to decentralized platforms and sanctioned entities.

IMF & World Bank. Discussed as lenders enforcing compliance through fiscal restructuring conditions (e.g., Argentina's 2022 deal, Ghana, Greece).

International Sustainability Standards Board. Referenced in climate narrative chapters for ESG coordination and scoring structures.

ISO / WTO / WIPO / ESG Frameworks. Mentioned across chapters as upstream compliance structures—used for credentialing access to global systems.

JCDecaux. (2024, April 23). *JCDecaux publishes the results of a study that measures the socioeconomic footprint of its activities worldwide and in France.* Retrieved from https://www.jcdecaux.com/press-releases/jcdecaux-publishes-results-study-measures-socioeconomic-footprint-its-activities

Mastercard & Doconomy. (2021–2023). Created carbon-tracking wallets and integrated programmable limits with central bank APIs.

Meta / Facebook. (2020–2023). Used mod logs and metadata in fusion center coordination and domestic behavioral surveillance.

ProPublica. (2024). Investigated therapy app data-sharing with insurers and marketing firms.

Singapore (2023). Piloted individual carbon budgets through national carbon credit allocation systems.

Skinner, B. F. (1957). *Schedules of Reinforcement.* Appleton-Century-Crofts.

Smith-Mundt Modernization Act (2013). Enabled U.S. government messaging to target domestic audiences.

Sur Journal. (2024). Documented opt-out rates, digital privacy resistance campaigns, and NGO funding declarations.

Toure-Tillery, M., & Fishbach, A. (2018). *How internal conflict and resolution shape moral judgment. Journal of Consumer Research*, 44(3), 499–512.

U.S. National Strategy for Countering Domestic Terrorism (2021). Cited in discussion of media-aligned domestic narrative enforcement.

UNDP (2024). "Data Resilience" platform coordinated with Mastercard, Meta, and WHO across 22 nations.

WEF (World Economic Forum). (2020–2024). Referenced in resilience indices, stakeholder capitalism reports, Known Traveler Digital Identity whitepapers, and ESG narrative frameworks.

Wikileaks (2015). Disclosed corporate influence in TPP drafts and intellectual property enforcement clauses.

YouTube (2024). Demonetization of mental health content under vague safety policy changes.

X (formerly Twitter). (2023). "Deboosting" documents revealed algorithmic suppression of critics.

About the Author

James "JiLm" Ergle is a political essayist, cartoonist, and investigator. Before writing this book, he worked as a capital murder mitigation specialist, private investigator, and contract disaster inspector. Before that, he was a grocery store manager, movie projectionist, liquor store clerk, powered wheelchair repairman, Blockbuster manager, interstate child support worker, and professional photographer. He has held just enough jobs to know how systems break people, and just enough power to know most of it is fake.

His writing focuses on the invisible scripts that govern modern life. He explores how institutions shape behavior, how power hides in policy, and how control gets sold as convenience. He combines firsthand experience with research-driven essays and biting cartoons to expose what most people have been trained not to see.

He does not write to reassure you. He writes to wake you up.

This is his second book.

You can read more at **radicalleanings.substack.com** or follow him on Threads at **@themagicmanjilm**

www.ingramcontent.com/pod-product-compliance
Lightning Source LLC
Chambersburg PA
CBHW070617030426
42337CB00020B/3833